Praise

As one who has [...] er-vation that *30 Days to Genesis* deserves nothing but praise and commendation. My Old Testament colleague Dr. Chet Roden has crafted a delightful study of the Bible's book of beginnings that combines accurate scholarship with solid application for today's Church. His heart, honed by many years shepherding a local church, shines through in this delightful book of devotional reflections that will both inform and challenge believers in their Christian walk.

—Dr. David D. Pettus
Associate Professor of Biblical Studies/Old Testament
Liberty University School of Divinity
Managing Editor, *Eruditio Ardescens*

Chet Roden has brought both his excellent scholarly skills and his pastor's passionate heart to life on the pages of *30 Days to Genesis*. He has masterfully opened up the biblical text and leads the reader to great spiritual truths. Not done there, Chet closes each devotional with "Food for Thought" to help us process God's revealed truth, "Faith in Action" to encourage us to be "doers" and not just "hearers" of the Word, and "Prayer" coaching to guide our time with the Master. *30 Days to Genesis* will change your life.

—Dr. Jim Parker
Professor of Biblical Interpretation
New Orleans Baptist Theological Seminary

As Christ followers, God calls us to read His Word for our personal growth. Reading a devotional resource that aids our understanding of Scripture can be a great blessing, too. In *30 Days to Genesis*, Dr. Roden has given us a tool to enrich our lives through God's Word. I would recommend that you buy and read this great book on Genesis. Thanks, Chet, for your investment in the lives of many believers through your labors.

—Dr. Michael A. Grisanti
Professor of Old Testament, Adjunct Instructor of Biblical Studies
The Master's Seminary

Dr. Roden's new book, *30 Days to Genesis*, does an excellent job of being true to the literary structure of the original Hebrew text of Genesis, while at the same time taking the events of this important book and making them real for the modern reader. I recommend that you get a copy and read it today!

—Dr. Steven M. Ortiz
Professor of Archaeology and Biblical Backgrounds,
School of Theology Director,
Charles D. Tandy Institute of Archaeology

The first book of the Bible is strategic for the Christian to understand, because it presents in seed form the major teachings of the entire Bible. What better way to enhance our understanding of Genesis than spending a month with the insightful daily devotional readings of *30 Days to Genesis*. In this daily devotional work, Dr. Chet Roden challenges us to grow spiritually as a result of each day's Bible reading. In today's world, where "spirituality without the Bible" is the norm, 30 Days to Genesis is a refreshing reminder that authentic discipleship only occurs when we submit our lives to the truth of Scripture. I encourage you to get this great new book!

—Dr. Larry Steven McDonald
Dean of Graduate School of Christian Ministry
and Director of DMin Studies, North Greenville University
Author, *Merging of Theology and Spiritual*
Co–Editor/Contributor to *Passion for the Great Commission*

30 DAYS TO
GENESIS

30 Days to Genesis
A Devotional Commentary

Chet Roden

Seed Publishing Group, LLC
Timmonsville, South Carolina

30 Days to Genesis: A Devotional Commentary

Copyright © 2016 by Chet Roden

Published by:
Seed Publishing Group
2570 Double C Farm Ln
Timmonsville, SC 29161
seed–publishing–group.com

Edited by:
Bill Curtis, Ph.D.
Dwayne Milioni, Ph.D.

All rights reserved. No part of this book may be reproduced or transmitted in any form or by any means, electronic or mechanical, including photocopying and recording, or by any information storage or retrieval system, except as may be expressly permitted in writing by the publisher. Requests for permission should be addressed in writing to Seed Publishing Group, LLC; 2570 Double C Farm Lane; Timmonsville, SC 29161.

Scripture quotations are from The Holy Bible, English Standard Version® (ESV®), copyright © 2001 by Crossway, a publishing ministry of Good News Publishers. Used by permission. All rights reserved.

To order additional copies of this resource visit www.seed–publishing–group.com.

Library of Congress Control Number: 2016940916

ISBN-13: 978-0-9968412-4-5

1 2 3 4 5 6 7 8 9 10

Printed in the United States of America

Dedication

In the broadest sense, I dedicate this book to my students and parishioners. Their listening ears have allowed me to rehearse and re-rehearse the messages I have found in Genesis. Through the recital of those passages, whether it be sermons and lessons, I have found Genesis to be a great source of strength and faith for my own spiritual journey. So, thanks to all of you who heard and prayed for me as I worked through Genesis.

Specifically, I dedicate the book to my wife, who has lovingly encouraged and supported my endeavors, often to the neglect of her own. Then I must mention my two sons and daughter-in-law, who have always seemed to understand when I needed to be some place besides with them. Lastly, I dedicate this to my soon to be born granddaughter. I hope one day this book will point you toward our wonderful Creator.

Contents

Foreword xiii
Preface xv

Day 1 The God Who Acts 1
       Genesis 1:1–2:3

Day 2 The Loss of Paradise 7
       Genesis 2:4–3:24

Day 3 Getting a Do-Over 13
       Genesis 4:1–26

Day 4 Death Dominates 19
       Genesis 5

Day 5 Sin Multiplies 25
       Genesis 6:1–8

Day 6 Chosen Traits 31
       Genesis 6:9–22

Day 7 In God We Trust 37
       Genesis 7:1–24

Day 8 Our Prevailing God 43
       Genesis 8:1–9:29

Day 9 God Loves Us 49
       Genesis 10:1–32

Day 10 Say What? 53
       Genesis 11:1–9

Day 11 Responding to God 59
       Genesis 11:10–12:20

Day 12 The Crucible of Faith 65
       Genesis 12:9–14:24

Day 13 How to Mess-up the Plan of God 71
       Genesis 15:1–16:16

Contents

Day 14 The Friend of God 77
Genesis 17:1–20:18

Day 15 The Day Laughter Came
to Abraham and Sarah 85
Genesis 21:1–24

Day 16 Abraham Offers Isaac Back to God 91
Genesis 22:1–25:11

Day 17 The Other Son Syndrome 97
Genesis 25:12–18

Day 18 Struggling for Position 103
Genesis 25:19–34

Day 19 Jacob's Web 109
Genesis 26:1–27:46

Day 20 Jacob's Harvest and God's Surprise 115
Genesis 28:1–35:55

Day 21 Jacob's Return 121
Genesis 32:1–35:29

Day 22 A View of the Land 127
Genesis 36:1–37:1 and Hebrews 11:8–16

Day 23 Joseph's Peril 133
Genesis 37:2–38:30

Day 24 Prosperity and the Slave 139
Genesis 39:1–41:57

Day 25 Extending God's Salvation 145
Genesis 42:1–45:28

Day 26 Following God Into Difficult Tasks 151
Genesis 46:1–34

Day 27 Learning to Bloom Where Planted 157
Genesis 47:1–31

Day 28 Facing Two Directions 163
Genesis 48:1–50:13

Day 29 Buried in Egypt, Longing for Home 169
Genesis 50:14–26

Day 30 A Certain God for Uncertain Times 175
Exodus 1:1–14

Finding L.I.F.E. in Jesus! 179

Foreword

Genesis is the book of beginnings. As such, it introduces the whole story of the Bible. In one sense it is the story of God. He speaks, creates, calls, chooses, blesses, promises, and visits His creation to intervene in human lives. On the other hand, Genesis is the story of people. We see them as they really were: Heroes and villains, patriarchs and matriarchs, the sons of God and daughters of men. We see them at their best and worst. Real people who lived in real history, whose stories still speak to us today.

Unlike ancient mythological literature, Genesis portrays its heroes as they really were, "worts and all," we might say. Abraham believes God one day and laughs at God another day. Sarah suggests a solution to a problem only to create a problem. We are introduced to raw human emotions of fear, failure, pain, and betrayal. Time and again, we are given a realistic glimpse of human nature in the ancient world.

Behind the pages of this inspired docudrama we see the hopes and dreams of men and women raised, dashed, and raised again. We are given a glimpse into the struggles of the human soul that allow us to transcend time, culture, and distance from the ancient world to our world. The very principles that spoke to Moses' original audience still speak to us today. It is these principles that Chet Roden has extracted in this moving and insightful devotional on the book of Genesis. In 30 succinct chapters Dr. Roden provides a guideline for our devotions as we explore the great truths of scripture and apply them to our daily lives.

Every chapter is written in an engaging style, laced with personal illustrations and practical applications. The

Foreword

readings include: Food for Thought, Faith in Action, and suggestions for Prayer. Each of these "pull outs" help us apply the ideas Chet is sharing with us. He has the mind of a scholar, the heart of a pastor, and the curiosity of an archaeologist. He will make you think, reflect, and dig for truth.

The advantage of the 30 day approach is that you can start at any point you choose. Obviously, the ideal would be to start at the beginning of the month. Nevertheless, you can start at any point you decide. The key is to get started, stick with it, and keep going. Each new day will build on the previous one. By the time you finish, you will begin to have a grasp on the most foundational book of the entire Bible. Even more, you will be challenged to apply some of the most basic and essential principles of living by faith in your journey with God as you walk in the path of the patriarchs with Dr. Roden as your guide.

—Dr. Ed Hindson
 Dean & Distinguished Professor School of Divinity
 Liberty University

Preface

Most scholars agree that Genesis is organized around the phrase "these are the generations of." The Hebrew word for generations is "toledoth." As a result, this phrase has become known as a "toledoth formula." There are ten of these statements throughout Genesis, which form eleven main sections of the book. These phrases represent transitions in Genesis which the author Moses used to organize his content. Below are the toledoth formulas in Genesis.

The Toledoth Formulas of Genesis

- Introduction and Creation 1:1–2:3
- Toledoth of the heavens and the earth 2:4–4:26
- Toledoth of Adam 5:1–6:8
- Toledoth of Noah 6:9–9:29
- Toledoth of the Sons of Noah 10:1–11:9
- Toledoth of Shem 11:10–26
- Toledoth of Terah 11:27–25:11
- Toledoth of Ishmael 25:12–18
- Toledoth of Isaac 25:19–35:29
- Toledoth of Esau 36:1–37:1
- Toledoth of Jacob 37:2–50:26

When we look at this list, we can see that the book of Genesis is a collection of family stories. As you proceed through the book, however, look for the way that God works through the lives of these families. God is the beginning and the end of this book. He is the main character; the one constant throughout the book. He creates, judges,

Preface

promises, protects, calls, and guides the narrative of Genesis. As the families of the earth expand, God directs his focus toward one family—the family of Jacob. As a result, the toledoth of Jacob occupies more space than any other family story in Genesis except for Terah's (Abraham's father).

Genesis is divided into two main sections. Scholars have long noted that the first eleven chapters deal with man's primeval history, while chapters 12–50 recount the stories of the biblical patriarchs. The devotions of this book will be loosely based upon the toledoths and this two–part structure of Genesis. While the daily readings will not openly stress them, those organizational structures will be the skeletal structure around which the devotions are formed. My prayer is that you will have a great thirty–day journey through Genesis.

One more thing . . . This book is part of a larger series of books that is being developed by Seed Publishing Group; it is called *30 Days to the Bible*. Each year, several new books will be added to this series until all the books of the Bible have been covered. Renowned scholars and pastors from around the country will be writing books for this exciting, new series. So, if you like *30 Days to Genesis*, keep your eyes open for the next books in the series: *30 Days to James*, *30 Days to Acts*, *30 Days to the Parables*, *30 Days to John*, and *30 Days to Colossians*!

Finally, Seed Publishing Group (www.seed–publishing–group.com) is an independent publisher committed to bringing great resources to both individual Christians and the local church. As part of that commitment, they are partners with The Pillar Network for church planting (www.thepillarnetwork.com). $1 from each sale of *30 Days to Genesis* goes directly to church plants throughout North America. Thank you for purchasing *30 Days to Genesis*, and thank you for investing in church planting!

—Dr. Chet Roden

Day 1

The God Who Acts

Genesis 1:1–2:3

God. That is where it all begins—with God. Before there was a human being, there was God. Before there was a planet, there was God. Before there was a sun in the sky, there was God. Before there was a beginning, there was God. Genesis begins with the simple fact that when the beginning began, God was there.

The Book of Genesis is often thought of as the book of beginnings. After all, it is the beginning book of the Bible. The first phrase of the first sentence says, "In the beginning." In Genesis, we discover many new things: the origin of different languages; the call of Abraham to be the father of many nations; the growth of the nation of Israel. Genesis is full of beginnings.

At its core, however, Genesis is a book about God. God's actions brought about all those beginnings. "In the beginning", God did something—he created. God caused THE beginning! The Hebrew word for "beginning" is actually one that means "head, top, or first." God is assumed to be at the "top, head, or first" of it all. Before the beginning, there was God.

Genesis 1:1 is clear that God created the heavens and the earth. The verse is a clear concise statement with little room for misunderstanding. So, God created matter; God created gases; God created the elements; God created atoms; God created molecules, electrons, protons, and

> *At its core, however, Genesis is a book about God.*

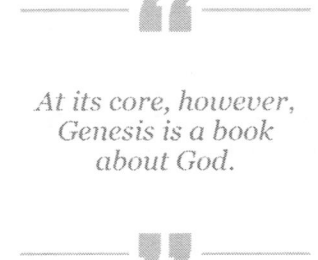

neutrons. Genesis simply proceeds from the assumption "In the beginning, God."

While beginnings are significant, the beginnings found in Genesis are merely a window into the character of the God, who began it all. Genesis invites us to read along and observe the character of God. From Genesis 1:1–2:3, God is mentioned 35 times in 34 verses. We can deduce the importance of God in this passage simply by counting the number of times he is mentioned.

More importantly, we learn something about God himself. First, God is an active God. He created, spoke, evaluated, made, named, established, blessed, saw, and sanctified. Despite the popular notion that God created the universe and left it to run itself, it is hard to imagine such an active God would suddenly become a "hands–off" type of God. God is active and engaged in his creation.

Second, God is a provider. The second half of chapter one reveals his provision. God provided man with many of his own attributes (i.e., the ability to think, reason, choose, feel, and speak). God provided man with purpose, "Be fruitful and multiply, and fill the earth and subdue it, and have dominion over . . . every living thing that moves on the earth (Gen 1:28)." God provided food for all living things on the earth. During creation, God revealed himself as a provider.

Thankfully, God still provides for his creatures. The apostle Paul reminds us of that truth in Philippians 4:19, "My God will supply all your needs according to his riches in glory in Christ Jesus." God is a great provider who supplies all of our needs.

Third, God enjoys his creation. After every day of creative activity, God looked at his work and declared that it was good! Genesis 1:31 says, "God saw all that he had made, and behold, it was *very* good [emphasis mine]." Did

Day 1

you catch that? It was very good. This Hebrew word implies an abundance of something.

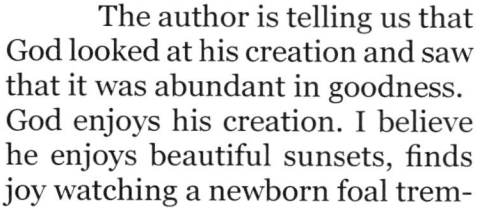

> *God is an active God.*

The author is telling us that God looked at his creation and saw that it was abundant in goodness. God enjoys his creation. I believe he enjoys beautiful sunsets, finds joy watching a newborn foal tremble and shake while attempting to stand for the first time, and is pleased by the melodies of songbirds in the morning. And, I believe that God enjoys you and me.

The psalmist David once wondered how such a great God could love humans like he does. David had been pondering the greatness of the heavens and the universe. After considering all of the wonderful works of God's hands, he asked an insightful question, "What is man that you are mindful of him and the son of man that you care for him? (Ps 8:4)." I don't think David is unique in his amazement at that thought.

I have been a pastor for many years, and I have counseled many people in countless situations. Often, God's people feel undeserving of God's love and favor. Sometimes this results from an ongoing battle with a stronghold of sin. Other times it results from a difficult trial in their lives. Regardless, the question is the same, "Who am I that God would love me?" Maybe you've asked that same question.

You're not alone. In the book of Romans, Paul wrote, "For while we were still weak, at the right time Christ died for the ungodly. . . . But God shows his love for us in that while we were still sinners, Christ died for us (Rom 5:6, 8)." When we were helpless, God showed his love for us through Jesus! Sure, we may disappoint God sometimes, but he

> *God is a great provider who supplies all of our needs.*

30 Days to Genesis

> *From Genesis to Revelation, the entire Bible shouts that God loves his creation; he loves you and me.*

loves and enjoys his creation, and that includes us!

The ultimate statement about God's loves for the people he created is found in John 3:16–17. Here John wrote, "For God so loved the world that he gave his only Son, that whoever believes in him should not perish but have eternal life. For God did not send his Son into the world to condemn the world, but in order that the world might be saved through him." From Genesis to Revelation, the entire Bible shouts that God loves his creation; he loves you and me.

Wow, what a great God! He was engaged in his creation, he provided for his creation, and he enjoyed his creation. You may ask, "But is God the same now? Does he still do that for his creation?" The answer is a resounding, "Yes!" Look at what the Psalmist wrote, "Of old you laid the foundation of the earth, and the heavens are the work of your hands. They will perish . . . but you are the same (Ps 102:25–27)." God is the same yesterday, today, and forever (Heb 13:8), and he is still sustaining his creation in every way (Heb 1:3).

What does that mean for us? It means God is willing to be engaged and involved in our lives. It means that God will provide for our needs when we call upon him. It means that God enjoys you and me. For us, that is very good.

Day 1

Food for Thought

Have you ever paused to consider that God enjoys you? Do you realize that God wants to be active in your life and wants to provide for you? Think about your relationship with God. Where is it today? Is your life bringing God joy or sorrow?

Faith in Action

Think of a few ways that God has been engaged in your life. Then, name at least one thing you know God has provided for you and thank him for it. Finally, do at least one thing today that would cause God to smile.

Prayer

If you have a particular need today, ask God to meet it. He desires to do so. If you're struggling to accept the truth that God loves you, ask him to help you feel his love and presence. If a sin in your life is hindering your fellowship with God, ask him to forgive you, so he can find joy in you today.

Day 2

The Loss of Paradise

Genesis 2:4–3:24

Let's be completely honest—humans sin. We know that our hearts are sinful, as is the world around us. In Ecclesiastes 7:20 we read, "Surely there is not a righteous man on earth who does good and never sins." In the New Testament Paul wrote, "For all have sinned and fall short of the glory of God (Rom 3:23)." We can agree with those statements on personal, experiential grounds. As a result, we cannot understand our world without understanding the origins of sin.

Genesis chapter two provides a more thorough, extended description of Genesis 1:26–27. In those verses, God decreed to create "man" in the general sense. There, the word "man" is the common term for mankind, including both male and female. In these two verses, we are given the God's concept of mankind, male and female beings designed in his image.

In Genesis 2:5, this being is simply called "man" (Hebrew "adam"). For the remainder of chapter two, the author includes the Hebrew definite article calling him "the man" and making the reference a bit more specific. But, it is interesting to note that this male person created by God, in his own image, is simply called "the man." The terminology, which is in the masculine form, is slightly

> *The serpent shifted the focus away from the freedom they had to eat from many trees and directed it towards the prohibition not to eat from one tree.*

more specific. It is not until later that this word becomes the name Adam.

Nonetheless, God formed the man (adam) out of the dust of the ground (Hebrew "adamah," Gen 2:7). Clearly, there is a play on words here (based on the similarity of the two Hebrew words). We read that God placed him in the garden called Eden to tend it. The man named the animals, but none of them were a "helper fit for him (Gen 2:18, 20)." God allowed the man to discover this on his own so that he would fully appreciate the woman that God would create for him. God formed her, not from the dust of the ground, the adamah, but from the man, adam. As a result, she was bone of his bone and flesh of his flesh. This woman was the one the man had been seeking within the garden. Yet until Genesis 3:20, she, like the man, is simply called "the woman."

There appeared to be a brief season when God's human creatures had not yet sinned. There they were, male and female, the crowning jewels of what God pronounced to be "very good (Gen 1:31)." Chapter two ends with a very pleasant synopsis, "And the man and his wife were both naked and were not ashamed (Gen 2:25)." Sadly, that soon changed.

Sin entered the world in a curious way—through the temptation of a serpent (Gen 3:1). The serpent brought into Eden the subtle threat of deception, and his target was Eve (Gen 3:13). He deceived her in three specific ways. First, the serpent tempted her to question the truthfulness of God's words. Notice how he confronted her with a propositional question, "Did God actually say, 'You shall not eat of any tree in the garden'?" The serpent was referring to Gen 2:16–17, where God gave the man and woman the freedom to eat from "every tree in the garden" with one

Day 2

exception: "Of the tree of the knowledge of good and evil you shall not eat."

We must note the difference between what God actually said and what the serpent claimed he said. There is a big difference. The serpent changed God's positive statement (You may eat from all of the fruit trees except one) into a negative statement (Did God really say you can't eat from any of the trees?). This shift was crafty and subtle. The serpent shifted the focus away from the freedom they had to eat from many trees and directed it towards the prohibition not to eat from one tree. Suddenly, Eve was thinking about how limited they were versus how free they were; she was focusing on the negative instead of the positive. The serpent caused her to question the truthfulness of God's words.

Second, the serpent challenged the trustworthiness of God's words. He told Eve, "You will not surely die (Gen 3:4)." However, God had specifically warned them, "In the day that you eat of it you shall surely die (Gen 2:17)." The serpent was defiantly challenging the reliability of God's word. We know that serpent was lying—death is all around us. But Eve had never experienced death in the garden. She had two choices: trust God's words or those of the serpent. Unfortunately for us, she made a terrible decision.

Third, the serpent tempted Eve to question the character of God. His final statement was the worst: "God knows that when you eat of it your eyes will be opened, and you will be like God, knowing good and evil (Gen 3:5)." The serpent tempted Eve with the notion that she could be a god. His trap was set. Eve now doubted God's truthfulness, trustworthiness, and character. The serpent insinuated that God was an insecure, power hungry, egotistical deity who refused to allow Adam and Eve to reach their true potential.

It's interesting to note that they already knew everything that

> *Once they ate from the prohibited tree, the idyllic setting of Eden crashed around them like a broken mirror.*

9

> *Sin entered the world because of the lustful desires and pride of our first ancestors.*

was good; all they had to gain was the knowledge of evil. Sadly, both Eve and Adam succumbed to the serpent's devious arguments. Eve ate from the tree and gave some to Adam, who was with her (Gen 3:6).

Once they ate from the prohibited tree, the idyllic setting of Eden crashed around them like a broken mirror. We are told, "Then the eyes of both of them were opened, and they knew that they were naked; and they sewed fig leaves together and made themselves loin coverings (Gen 3:7)." Shame and guilt washed over them like a flood, and God drove them from the garden because of their rebellion. This was the original Paradise Lost.

In 1 John 2:15–17, John may have had Eden in mind when he wrote, "Do not love the world or the things in the world. If anyone loves the world, the love of the Father is not in him. For all that is in the world – the desires of the flesh and the desires of the eyes and pride of life – is not from the Father but is from the world. And the world is passing away along with its desires, but whoever does the will of God abides forever."

The similarities are evident. The fleshly lusts of Eve and Adam caused them to questioned God's will. They looked at the tree and lusted for its fruit. Their boastful pride, aroused by the crafty questions of the serpent, made them desire to be a god. None of those desires came from the Father.

Sin entered the world because of the lustful desires and pride of our first ancestors. We could blame them for the sinful state of our world, but we shouldn't. We would have done the same thing as Eve and Adam if we were in their situation.

> *God wants us to live with faith in his will for our lives—it is always good!*

Day 2

James, the brother of Jesus, gave us an important warning. He wrote, "But each person is tempted when he is lured and enticed by his own desire. Then desire when it has conceived gives birth to sin, and sin when it is fully grown brings forth death. Do not be deceived, my beloved brothers (James 1:14–16)." We are tempted to sin in many ways every day. Like Eve and Adam, we are tempted to question God's truthfulness, trustworthiness, and character. When we disobey God, it harms both us, and often the people around us. Instead, God wants us to live with faith in his will for our lives—it is always good!

Food for Thought

Have you ever realized that sin is not accidental? Think about your own life. Are you tempted by certain sins? Think about how those temptations cause you to question God's truthfulness, trustworthiness, and character. Sin is punishable because it is a willful action against God and his commands. Sin is never an accident.

Faith in Action

Identify the sins you struggle with the most (pride, anger, greed, lust, frustration, bitterness, a critical spirit, vile speech, etc.). What does the Bible say about those sins? Agree with God about those sins and the damage they can cause in your life.

Prayer

Talk with the sins that easily capture you. Ask God to forgive you for your willingness to tolerate those sins in your heart. Ask God to help you trust his word and give you the strength to obey it. Thank God for the warnings in his word that can help you avoid the harsh consequences of sin.

Day 3

Getting a Do–Over

Genesis 4:1–26

Do–overs are great, aren't they? When we really mess something up, the opportunity to do that thing again, and do it correctly, can be a precious commodity. I cannot count the number of times I've wanted a do–over in my life. I guess that's why I love computers. I can write as my thoughts flow freely. Then, if what I've written is poor, I hit the delete key, and I get a do–over!

Genesis four describes the results of Eve and Adam's tragic act of rebellion against God. Interestingly, the chapter is presented to us as a do–over story. Typically, we associate this chapter with Cain and Abel. It is here we find the famous saying, "Am I my brother's keeper?" By the end of the chapter, however, we realize that it's a story of hope; hope for correcting the mess created by the fall—it's a do–over story.

If we focus on the Cain and Abel story alone, we will miss the main point of the chapter. Chapter four flows seamlessly out of the story of Adam and Eve's punishment and banishment from Eden. As God was cursing the serpent he said, "I will put enmity between you and the woman, and between your offspring and her offspring; he shall bruise your head, and you shall bruise his heel (Gen 3:15)." According to Genesis 3:16, childbirth would be painful, but Eve knew that she would one day have a child, her offspring, which would bruise the head of the serpent. She could foresee a do–over opportunity on the horizon.

> *The consequences of sin are always greater than anticipated.*

Genesis 4:1 states that Adam and Eve had a child, and Eve named him Cain. She then exclaimed, "I have gotten a man with the help of the Lord." Eve's statement is one of great joy and anticipation. This was a child "from the Lord." She must have been thinking, "This is the child God told us about. He is the one who will bruise the head of the serpent; the one that caused all this of this mess. This is the chance to correct my mistake. This is a do-over. Excitement must have radiated throughout their home."

In verse two, we are told that Eve had another child, who was also a son; she named him Abel. Perhaps he might bruise the head of the serpent. Cain was a farmer like his daddy, while Abel was a shepherd. Although they were no longer in the garden, they were settling into the "new normal" of a world plagued by sin. Adam and Eve would soon understand that the consequences of sin are always greater than anticipated.

In Genesis 4:3, the story of Adam and Eve is interrupted by the phrase, "It happened in the course of time." This is a transitional phrase that serves two purposes. First, it pauses the Adam and Eve story, which will resume in Genesis 4:25, and marks the beginning of another story about Cain and his family. Second, the phrase works as a conjunction that links the Adam and Eve story with the story of Cain (Gen 4:3–24).

From the beginning of the Cain narrative, we recognize his inability to bruise the head of the serpent. When God rejected Cain's offering of farm produce, his unrestrained anger was apparent. God warned Cain about his anger and told him that he must master it before it destroyed him (Gen 4:6–7). Cain refused to listen, choosing instead to let his anger control him.

Abel, on the other hand, brought God an acceptable offering—a lamb. As a result, Cain's anger burned strongly

Day 3

against his brother. This is curious to me. Cain brought his offering to God, and it was God who rejected it. Yet, Cain was angry with Abel, even though he had nothing to do with Cain's problem.

Rather than being angry at himself for bringing the wrong offering, or even at God for not accepting his offering, Cain was angry at Abel because his brother's offering was accepted by God. Jealousy fueled Cain's anger, and he blamed Abel rather than confessing his sin and bringing God an acceptable offering. Like his parents before him, Cain was about to learn that the consequences of sin are always greater than anticipated.

What follows was a tragic event—Cain killed Abel. God confronted Cain about his sin in much the same way that he confronted Adam and Eve about their sins. And, he placed a curse upon Cain also. God cursed Cain saying, "You are cursed from the ground . . . you shall be a fugitive and a wanderer on the earth (Gen 4:11–12)." Because of his refusal to bring the correct offering, God was never going to allow Cain to succeed as a farmer again. Cain exclaimed, "My punishment is greater than I can bear (v. 13)!" God had warned him, but Cain had not anticipated such a painful consequence.

As time passed and Cain's family grew, sin continued to ravage God's good creation. Five generations later, Lamech became the face of Cain's family; sadly, Lamech was shameless in his sin. He was the first to take multiple wives (Gen 4:19). Then, he murdered a young man who had attacked him (Gen 4:23). And, as if that escalation of sin was not enough, Lamech egotistically boasted, "If Cain's revenge is sevenfold, then Lamech's is seventy–sevenfold (Gen 4:24)." He was neither remorseful nor concerned about his grievous sins. He was more concerned that people recognize his "greater than Cain" status.

The Cain narrative ends with the escalation of sin and its consequences. Cain, the son Eve once hoped would be the promised offspring who would bruise the head of the serpent, was instead the father of a sinful and death–

> *Sin is far more volatile and deadly than we may think, and its consequences are much greater than we can imagine.*

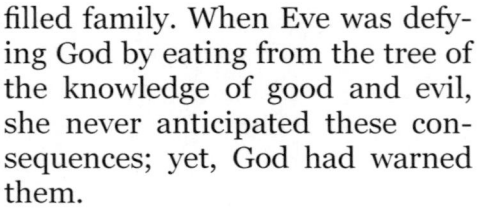

filled family. When Eve was defying God by eating from the tree of the knowledge of good and evil, she never anticipated these consequences; yet, God had warned them.

Adam and Eve's story resumes in Genesis 4:25. We are told that they had another son and named him Seth, because "God has appointed for me another offspring instead of Abel, for Cain killed him (Gen 4:25)." The Hebrew word translated "offspring" is the same one we observed in Genesis 3:15, where Eve was promised a son who would bruise the head of the serpent. It seems that Eve viewed the birth of Seth as another opportunity to defeat the serpent and correct the awful effects of sin. Cain had failed; he was the father of a sinful, killing line. Abel wasn't the one either, because Cain had killed him. The birth of Seth was another do–over opportunity

With the birth of Seth and his son Enosh, "People began to call upon the name of the Lord (Gen 4:26)." Cain's family and descendants never called upon the name of the Lord. Seth's family was different; they were God–fearers. Seth's lineage discovered that sin couldn't be corrected through human effort—they needed God's help.

Sin is far more volatile and deadly than we may think, and its consequences are much greater than we can imagine. Like Seth's family, we need God's help to overcome sin in our lives.

Day 3

Food for Thought

Think about a time when sin had a serious consequence in your life or that of your family. How did that sin take root? What choices produced the painful consequence? What long-term affects have resulted in your life or that of your family? Now, consider how the decision to fear God (by accepting his truthfulness, trustworthiness, and character traits) might have changed that sinful trajectory in your life or family.

Faith in Action

Thankfully, God is always ready to give us a do-over when it comes to our sin. In 1 John 1:9 we read, "If we confess our sins, he is faithful and just to forgive us our sins and to cleanse us from all unrighteousness." Remember, God always forgives sin, but he doesn't promise to remove consequences. That said, it's never too late to chart a new course for our lives and our families. Today, imagine what your life would look like if you were intentional about trusting God's word and surrendering to his will for your life. Talk to your pastor today if you need help with this.

Prayer

In your prayer time today, talk with God about the sins you battle most. God saved you to give you victory over sin and its consequences in your life. Ask God to help you choose obedience in that area of your life today.

Day 4

Death Dominates

Genesis 5

John Donne once wrote, "Each man's death diminishes me, for I am involved in mankind. Therefore, send not to know for whom the bell tolls, it tolls for thee (Devotions Upon Emergent Occasions: Meditation XVII, 1624)." Genesis 5 is known notoriously as the death chapter. Death dominates it. Eight times we read the phrase "and he died." Death came because of sin, just as God had warned in Genesis 2:17. The repetitive tolling of the phrase "and he died" reminds us of Donne's famous statement about death: "It tolls for thee."

As I noted in the preface, the Toledoth of the heavens and the earth explained the origin of sin in the world and that its consequences are much greater than anticipated (Gen 2:4–4:26). The second half of that toledoth presented the hope for a do-over that would correct sin and overcome its consequences. Sadly, the results were dismal. Sin continued to escalate on earth.

The extent of sin's consequences come into clear focus with the Toledoth of Adam

> *God created Adam in his image, and in turn Adam had sons and daughters that bore his image as human beings. God created Adam and Eve without sin and gave them the free will to choose to obey him. When they rebelled against him and sinned, they caused all of their descendants to be born in their fallen image as sinners.*

19

(Gen 5:1– 6:8) and reveals his legacy: the first is a legacy of death; the second is a legacy of sin. Obviously, neither is desirable.

Adam's Toledoth provides us with a recap of creation. Genesis 5:1–2 reminds us that in the beginning God had created Adam in his likeness (Gen 1:26). Then, verse three reveals something interesting: Adam brought forth a son "in his own likeness, after his image, and named him Seth." A stark contrast is being drawn here. God created Adam in his image, and in turn Adam had sons and daughters that bore his image as human beings. God created Adam and Eve without sin and gave them the free will to choose to obey him. When they rebelled against him and sinned, they caused all of their descendants to be born in their fallen image as sinners. They doomed all of them to death, both physically and spiritually. From that moment to this, the tolling of the bell began to ring loudly as sinful man produced sinful man, and death produced death.

Adam lived 930 years and died; Seth lived 912 years and died; Enosh lived 905 years and died; Kenan lived 910 years and died; Mahalalel lived 895 years and died; Jared lived 962 years and died; Enoch lived 65 years, fathered Methuselah, and walked with God (Gen 5:21–22). Wait. What? The death bell had been ringing with such regularity that we expected it again— "and he died." According to the writing pattern used by the author in this chapter, we expect Enoch to live a certain number of years, beget sons, and die. But Enoch walked with God, so there is a different ending.

There was no ringing of the death bell for Enoch. The text says simply, "Enoch walked with God, and he was not, for God took him (Gen 5:24)." All that is mentioned is this matter–of–fact statement: "God took him." Wow! The tolling of the death bell missed a beat.

Genesis never mentions Enoch again. In fact, we must go to the New Testament in order to learn more about him. Enoch is mentioned in Hebrews 11, which is often called "The Hall of Fame of Faith." Hebrews 11:5–6

Day 4

says, "By faith Enoch was taken up so that he should not see death, and he was not found, because God had taken him. Now before he was taken he was commended as having pleased God. And without faith it is impossible to please him, for whoever would draw near to God must believe that he exists and that he rewards those who seek him." Enoch walked with God and pleased him because of his faith.

Just like his ancestor Seth, who began to call on the name of the Lord, Enoch had faith in God, and it pleased him. It pleased God so much that God suspended the tolling of the death bell for Enoch—God just took him. The word used in Hebrews for "taken" is the word from which our words "metathesis" and "metamorphosis" originate. God transferred Enoch from one realm to another, from the realm of earth and death to the realm of heaven and life.

Because of his faith in God, Enoch became an example for all Christians. Obviously, Enoch didn't know about Jesus Christ, the Messiah of Israel and the Savior of the Church. Still, in a culture of death, Enoch believed in God, walked with God, and was taken up to be with God because of it. As a result, he is an example for us in faith.

Let me explain. First, to become a Christian, we are asked to respond to Jesus in faith. John 3:16 says, "For God so loved the world that he gave his only Son, that whoever believes in him should not perish but have eternal life." Faith is the first step in becoming a Christian. We must believe that Jesus is the Christ, the Son of God, and that he died for our sins and was raised to life according to the Scriptures (If you've never placed your faith in Jesus Christ as your Savior and Lord, please pause here to read "Finding L.I.F.E. in Jesus!" in the Appendix of this book).

Second, Christians are urged to walk with God through obedience. In his writings to the

> *Faith is the first step in becoming a Christian.*

30 Days to Genesis

> As followers of Christ, we must walk with God and please him.

Thessalonians Paul wrote, "Finally, then, brothers, we ask and urge you in the Lord Jesus, that as you received from us how you ought to walk and to please God, just as you are doing, that you do so more and more (1 Thess. 4:1)." Here, Paul has joined the two concepts found in the life of Enoch – walking with God and pleasing him. As followers of Christ, we must walk with God and please him.

Third, when people place their faith Jesus Christ for salvation and begin to walk with him, they can expect to be changed in the same ways as Enoch. In his first letter to the Corinthians Paul wrote, "We shall not all sleep [die], but we shall all be changed, in a moment, in the twinkling of an eye, at the last trumpet. For the trumpet will sound, and the dead will be raised imperishable, and we shall be changed . . . then shall come to pass the saying that is written: 'Death is swallowed up in victory.' O death, where is your victory? O death, where is your sting . . . But thanks be to God, who gives us the victory through our Lord Jesus Christ (1 Cor 15:51–57)." Despite the fact that death still dominates our world, Christians can look forward to being changed one day. At the return of Christ, those who have died in the Lord will be resurrected with glorified bodies, while those who are living will be taken and transformed into glorified bodies also. Both groups will be changed in an instant, and both will be transferred from this world of sin and death into the heavenly world of a sinless eternity with God.

God has shown us the results of a life of faith from the beginning of time: "Enoch walked with God and he was not, for God took him (Gen 5:24)." Let me encourage you to follow Enoch's example. If you have not yet done so, commit your life to Christ through faith. Then, walk with God and live your life for his glory. That is the life that God rewards!

Day 4

Food for Thought

God rewards those who have a personal relationship with him through faith. Are you living a life of faith today? Do you trust that God's will for your life is best? Do you believe the principles God has given you through his word? Are you striving to allow God's character to be reflected in your life? The things are necessary in your life if you would please God and have his favor.

Faith in Action

Identify one area of your life where you need to grow in your faith in God. It may be related to overcoming a sin in your life. Maybe you need to trust what God says about developing a healthy marriage. Perhaps God wants you to share the gospel with one of your unsaved friends. Or, God may be leading you to become obedient in your stewardship by tithing to your church. Is God calling you to serve him in vocational ministry? Once you have identified one of these areas or perhaps something else, commit your heart to walk by faith in this area.

Prayer

In your prayer time today, talk with God about your struggles with faith. Are you afraid to follow God? If so, talk with him about the reasons. Do you know something that God wants you to do; yet, you're refusing to do it? Confess that sin and ask God for the courage to obey him.

Day 5

Sin Multiplies

Genesis 6:1–8

The awful death legacy of Adam is followed by an increasing multiplication of sin. In Genesis 6:1–7, we read that the situation got so bad that the Lord God was grieved that he had even created man. Genesis 6:5 is a very revealing text. "The Lord saw that the wickedness of man was great in the earth, and that every intention of the thoughts of his heart was only evil continually." Man's actions were wicked, but the wickedness went to his very core—into his heart. The text says, "Every intention of the thoughts of his heart was only evil continually [emphasis mine]." In just a few generations, the descendants of Adam had become sinners extraordinaire. Because of the rebellion of Adam and Eve, sin was multiplying at a rate that grieved the heart of God.

Today's text reveals three key ideas about the multiplication of sin. First, the multiplication of sin abbreviated that generation's time on earth (Gen 6:1–3). With the birth of Seth, family lines were drawn. There was the ungodly line of Cain (Gen 4:3–24) and the godly line of Seth (Gen 4:26). The demarcation between the two lines is seen in the phrase, "At that time people began to call upon the name of the Lord (Gen 4:26)." The descendants of Cain are never described like this. We read in Genesis 6:1–2 that the sons of God (who were from the lineage of Seth) began to intermarry with the daughters of man (who were from the lineage of Cain). God was upset and said, "My Spirit shall not abide in man forever (Gen 6:3)." The word "abide" literally means, "to contend." Basically, God was tired of wrestling with man. As a result, God gave man a timeline. Genesis 6:3 states, "His days shall be 120 years." Today, we know Noah's story so well that once he is introduced in Genesis 5:29, we anticipate the end of the story. But at this point in the Genesis narrative, the reader has not been told what is coming at the end of the 120 years. We are just told man's days are ending in 120 years.

In Genesis 5:32 we are told that Noah was 500 years old when he became the father of his sons. Then, in Genesis 7:6 we are told that Noah was 600 years old when the flood came. So, Noah was 480 years old when God made the decision to limit man's days. God was tired of mankind's sin, so a judgment flood was coming in 120 years.

Second, the multiplication of sin activated God's sorrow. Genesis 6:6 uses two different words to describe his sorrow. The text states that God "regretted" that he had made man. The Hebrew word for regret is one that is most often used in a passive form. It is a reaction verb; the action happens to the subject as a result of some situation. In this case, the multiplying sin of man activated God's feelings of sorrow, grief, and regret.

The other word, here translated "it grieved him," is a reflexive verb, which means that the subject is acting upon itself. God was grieved in his own heart. While God is transcendent and above human emotions as we know them, the author of Genesis was limited to the use of human language. So, he tried to describe God's feelings using human words. He wrote, "The Lord regretted that he had made man on the earth, and it grieved him to his heart (Gen 6:6)."

In order to alleviate the grief and eliminate the sin problem, God determined, "I will blot out man . . . and animals and creeping things and birds of the heavens, for I am sorry that I have made them (Gen 6:7)." Death had been dominating and sin had been multiplying, so God determined to end man's time on earth in 120 years. The

Day 5

Toledoth of Adam does not end at Genesis 6:7, however. The tragic end of Adam's legacy actually points us toward a better day.

Genesis 6:8 says, "But Noah found favor in the eyes of the Lord." Noah was introduced in Genesis five, but little was said about him at that time. His father Lamech named him Noah, saying, "Out of the ground that the Lord has cursed, this one shall bring us relief from our work and from the painful toil of our hands (Gen 5:29)." This brings the idea of the promised Seed back to our minds. When Cain was born, Eve thought he would be the promised Seed to crush the head of the serpent—he wasn't. Seth was also thought to be the promised Seed—he wasn't. Instead, his lineage grew more sinful because they born into the sin of their first ancestor Adam. In Noah, however, the idea of the promised Seed resurfaces.

The idea of Noah as the promised Seed is seen in another way that we may miss in our English translation of the Bible. The word for "favor" in Genesis 6:8 is the Hebrew word "khan," pronounced with a long "a" sound like "hay." Say it out loud. Hear what we miss? The Hebrew word for favor and grace sounds very similar to the name of Adam and Eve's firstborn son Cain. In Hebrew the two words sound a bit different, but their pronunciations are similar enough for the reader to recognize the play on words. The author could have used other words to speak of God's grace and mercy. Instead, he chose this word to make a special point. Noah found "khān" in the eyes of the Lord.

Clearly, the reader is to be reminded of the promised Seed. That Seed, however, would not be come the lineage of Cain, but would arise from God's "khān" through the line of Seth and Noah. In this Toledoth of death and sin, the importance of God's grace is amplified. Death was dominat-

> *God's grace is powerful enough to overcome the consequences of our sin.*

27

30 Days to Genesis

> *God's grace is sufficient to eradicate all of sin's consequences for any person who will receive it by faith in Jesus Christ.*

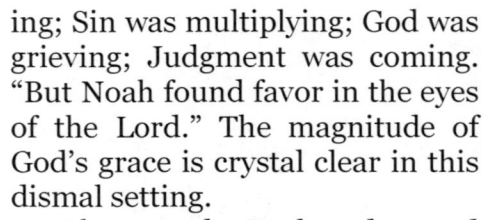

ing; Sin was multiplying; God was grieving; Judgment was coming. "But Noah found favor in the eyes of the Lord." The magnitude of God's grace is crystal clear in this dismal setting.

The apostle Paul understood this concept. In the Book of Romans he wrote, "Where sin increased, grace abounded all the more, so that, as sin reigned in death, grace also might reign through righteousness leading to eternal life through Jesus Christ our Lord (Rom 5:20–21)." God's grace is powerful enough to overcome the consequences of our sin. Sin cannot multiply beyond the limits of God's grace, and death cannot overpower it. God's grace is sufficient to eradicate all of sin's consequences for any person who will receive it by faith in Jesus Christ.

Day 5

Food for Thought

Have you ever thought about how our sin grieves the heart of the Father? Today, think about the things in your life that may be grieving the heart of God. Why are you allowing them to remain in your life? Also, think about how the grace of God can provide both forgiveness and deliverance from those sins. Isn't it great to know that our God is a God of grace?

Faith in Action

Now that you've identified some things in your life that grieve God's heart, consider what God's word has to say about them. Look in the concordance of your Bible for those things and read what the Bible has to say about them. What decisions should you make today based on God's word?

Prayer

In your prayer time today, talk with God about the things in your life that grieve his heart. Ask him to reveal why they have such a stronghold in your life, and the decisions you can make to minimize their hold on your heart. Finally, ask him to forgive you and help you overcome them in your life today.

Day 6

Chosen Traits

Genesis 6:9–22

As a musician, I love instruments. Through the years I've owned five guitars, two bass guitars, a trumpet, a mandolin, numerous keyboards, drums, a piano, and a variety of other assorted instruments. In particular, I love to play banjos. In fact, I've owned at least ten! My current banjo has become my favorite instrument of all time. It has all of the characteristics I want: it's sturdy, loud, clear, easy to play, and beautiful. Playing that instrument brings me great joy. I love it!

In today's text, we are going to examine some of the traits that God likes to see in the people he chooses to use for specific tasks—Noah was one of those people. At the close of the Toledoth of Adam, we read about a very sinful population. They had no remorse for sin, refused to listen to God, and rejected repentance. Yet Noah, who was introduced near the end of the Adam Toledoth, found grace in the eyes of the Lord (Gen 6:8).

In Genesis 6:9, the Toledoth of Noah begins and becomes the starting point for our study today. It begins by describing Noah and his character. Today, let's consider the characteristics of a person God uses for his glory.

First, Noah was righteous. The Hebrew word translated "righteous" specifies a person who is just in his or her conduct toward God and man. Also, it indicates a person with a righteous character. In other words, Noah was righteous, and it allowed him to behave justly and rightly towards God and others.

> God works through those who walk closely with Him.

Second, Noah was blameless in his generation. The word translated "blameless" here does not mean "sinless." Rather, it describes a wholesome quality of life. Noah was sound in judgment. He was not overcome by a sinful lifestyle; he was a man of integrity. Notice that the text says, Noah was blameless "in his generation." That was an amazing feat in the day in which Noah lived. Genesis 6:11 states, "The earth was corrupt in God's sight, and the earth was filled with violence." It is impossible to escape this comparison between Noah's righteous and blameless character and the sinful generation in which he lived. God chose to use a man who had remained righteous and blameless despite the sinful context in which he lived.

Third, Noah walked with God. Does that remind you of anyone? Remember, Enoch had walked with God also. In Scripture we observe that God works through those who walk closely with Him. While the text is silent about this, I believe that Noah's righteous and blameless character was a direct result of his walk with God, and God chose to use him in a great way because of their relationship.

Jesus spoke about this truth by using an illustration from a vineyard. He said, "I am the vine; you are the branches. Whoever abides in me and I in him, he it is that bears much fruit, for apart from me you can do nothing (Jn 15:5)." Abiding is synonymous with walking with God, and that's what Noah did. If we apply Jesus' analogy to Noah's situation, God was the vine, and Noah was the branch. The fruit Noah bore was a righteous and blameless life. In turn, this led to the fruit of preserving human and animal life on the ark.

Fourth, Noah was close enough to God that he could hear his voice. As Noah walked with God, he learned

Day 6

of God's plans to destroy the earth with a great flood. God told Noah that he was "determined to make an end of all flesh (Gen 6:13)." Can you imagine the fear and worry that must have filled Noah's mind?

As God revealed his plan, Noah learned that his family, and certain pairs of animals, would be spared. God told Noah, "Make yourself an ark of gopher wood (Gen 6:14)." I'm sure it was at this point that Noah's fears subsided. The ark would be the vehicle of their survival. God explained how Noah should build the ark and how he should supply it. Through this process God was revealing his plan to save a small remnant of humanity. God explained, "I will establish my covenant with you, and you shall come into the ark, you, your sons, your wife, and your son's wives with you. And of every living thing of all flesh, you shall bring two of every sort into the ark to keep them alive with you (Gen 6:18–19)."

Fifth, Noah obeyed God. Genesis 6:22 says, "Noah did this; he did all that God commanded him." There is no record of Noah arguing with God about the task or attempting to give him advice for building the ark. The people God uses are those who are willing to obey his will. Jesus himself demonstrated complete obedience when He prayed to his Father, "Not my will, but yours, be done (Lk 22:42)." Building the ark would be a difficult task; the stakes were incredibly high. But Noah did it. He did everything that God commanded him to do.

In the narrative flow of Genesis, we cannot neglect the fact that Noah becomes another potential man who could be the promised SEED; the one who would crush the head of the serpent. All of the other candidates had failed, and as a result, death dominated and sin multiplied in Noah's generation. As Genesis six closes, hope has been rekindled, even in the face of the coming worldwide catastrophe. God had chosen to use a man

> *The people God uses are those who are willing to obey his will.*

as a rescuer. He didn't just use any man, however. Noah was the man who found grace in the eyes of the Lord. He was a righteous and blameless man. He was a man who walked with God and learned to hear and obey his voice. Noah was a man who was willing to do everything that God commanded. God's work through Noah would save humanity. As Genesis six closes, we are left to wonder if Noah might be the promised SEED.

Day 6

Food for Thought

Have you ever thought that God wants to use you as an instrument of his will? I feel certain that he won't ask you to build an ark—after all, there's only one Noah. Still, God does want to use all of us, and he has a special, Kingdom purpose for your life. Are you walking with God today? Are you allowing God to speak to you through today's study? Are you trying to live a righteous and obedient life? The fact that you're reading this book means that you want that. Rejoice in this today—God will use you in amazing ways to further the gospel in his world.

Faith in Action

Do you want to be used by God to accomplish great things in his Kingdom? If so, strive to live the same principles that Noah did:
 1. Live a righteous life;
 2. Live a blameless life;
 3. Walk with God;
 4. Know God and listen to his word;
 5. Obey God.

Write these five concepts on a note card and place it where you can see it every day. Allow these principles to serve as motivation for your daily walk in Christ.

Prayer

In today's prayer time, talk with God about the principles that defined Noah's life. Ask him to give you a heart to pursue those things as well. Confess any sins that are hindering this pursuit, and ask for God's help in knowing, loving, and serving him in righteousness and obedience.

Day 7

In God We Trust

Genesis 7:1–24

Most of us go to work every day to earn an income to support our families' daily needs. When possible, we buy insurance for our accidents, save money for a "rainy day," and invest in some sort of retirement plan for the future. God provided all of those things for Noah and his family. God provided for his daily needs, protected him from the "rainy days" of the flood, and prepared for his future.

It occurred to me when reading this story that the author used a bunch of prepositions to tell this story. Prepositions are an oft overlooked, but important component, of the English language. When I was a youngster, I was taught that a preposition was "anything an airplane could do to a cloud." It could go in, out, above, below, through, around, etc. In Genesis 7, prepositions not only play a significant role in our understanding of the text, but also they play a significant role in our understanding of the actions of God, Noah, the animals, and the storm.

First, let's consider prepositions that speak to the intent of God. God told Noah, "Go into the ark (Gen 7:1)." His instructions were specific. Noah, his family, and the animals were not to be outside the ark, but in it. His reasons were just as specific. God said, "I will send rain on the earth forty days and forty nights, and every living thing that I have made I will blot out from the face of the ground (Gen 7:4)." This small group was to go into the ark because God planned to destroy the violent and sinful population.

> *This small group was to go into the ark because God planned to destroy the violent and sinful population.*

Two small prepositions make a huge impact in the flood story. The simple proposition, as stark as it might be, was this: Be 'in' the ark or you will be 'blotted out.' Once the preposition "out" was added to form the verb translated "blot," the action became fatal and terminal. Noah was to be in the ark to avoid God's lethal judgment on the sinful population.

Second, let's look at another preposition that reveals Noah's response to the impending judgment. Noah did everything that the Lord commanded him (Gen 7:5). He built the ark and gathered the animals. Then, "Noah and his sons and his wife and his sons' wives with him went into the ark to escape the waters of the flood (Gen 7:7)." Noah and his family went "into" the ark so that they would be saved.

Next, we are told that the animals "went into the ark with Noah, as God had commanded Noah (Gen 7:9, 15)." Then, we are told again that Noah and his family entered the ark (Gen 7:13). They went "in." The author was making it abundantly clear that Noah accomplished his role in God's plan. Noah, his family, and the animals went "into" the ark. They acted properly in response to God's judgment. God had given them a way of escape; they heeded his warning and went into the ark.

Third, let's think about the flood and the way that it is described by prepositions. "The flood continued forty days on the earth . . . and it rose high 'above' the earth (Gen 7:17)." Genesis 7:18 says that the flood "prevailed and increased greatly 'on' the earth." In Genesis 7:20 we read that the flood waters prevailed "above" the mountains fifteen cubits (22.5 feet). Finally, Genesis 7:24 says, "And the waters prevailed 'on' the earth 150 days." Clearly, these prepositions are meant to convince us that the floodwaters prevailed "on" and "above" the earth, the mountains, the animals, and all of humanity. The summary verse, Genesis

Day 7

7:23, is a grim one. God used the prevailing floodwaters to destroy "every living thing that was on the face of the ground, man and animals and creeping things and birds of the heavens. They were blotted out from the earth (Gen 7:23)."

Fourth, let's consider the prepositions that speak to the work of God. When the flood began, Noah, his family, and the animals "went in as God had commanded him (Gen 7:16)." Notice the next sentence carefully—it's one of the most important uses of a preposition in the entire story. The author writes, "And the Lord shut him in." Wow! Noah, his family, and the animals went in, but God shut them in! God did not shut them "out"; he shut them "in." God sealed the door behind them. Noah and his sons may have closed the door, but it was God who sealed them inside by his own sovereign power. From that point on, they were inside God's vehicle of protection.

Fifth, let's consider the response of the ark to the prevailing floodwaters. We read, "The waters increased and bore 'up' the ark, and it rose high 'above' the earth (Gen 7:17)." Imagine the raging and rising waters. The rains came down, and the water tables broke open, so that flood waters prevailed on the earth more than 22 feet above the highest mountains. Yet, God's protective vehicle rose higher. No matter how high the waters rose, the ark rose above them, riding the waves that prevailed over the mountains. Genesis 7:18 describes this scene in a powerful way: "The waters prevailed and increased greatly on the earth, and the ark floated 'on' the face of the waters." The waters prevailed on the earth, but God's vehicle of protection prevailed on the waters.

The good news for us today is that we find this theme of God's protective grace throughout the Bible. God offers it to his people over and over again. In one of his songs, the psalmist said, "He who dwells in the shelter of the

> *Noah and his family went "into" the ark so that they would be saved.*

39

> *God sent Jesus as the means of our salvation from eternal judgment. All those who believe in Jesus will have eternal life.*

Most High will abide in the shadow of the Almighty. I will say to the Lord, 'My refuge and my fortress, my God, in whom I trust.' (Ps 91:1–2)."

Paul taught about the theme of God's protective grace, as well. He wrote of Jesus, "In Him, you also, when you heard the word of truth, the gospel of your salvation, and believed in him, were sealed with the promised Holy Spirit, who is the guarantee of our inheritance until we acquire possession of it (Eph 1:13–14)." We are saved when we place our faith "in" Jesus. This is reminiscent of the Noah story. Warned by God of a coming judgment, Noah and his family believed God, accepted his protective grace, went into the ark, and were saved. Paul described those who believe in Jesus as being "sealed" eternally with the promised Holy Spirit. God saves them and secures them forever!

God sent Jesus as the means of our salvation from eternal judgment. All those who believe in Jesus will have eternal life. Have you entered that ark of protective grace that God has provided for you through Jesus?

Day 7

Food for Thought

Have you ever felt like life was overwhelming you? Today, reflect of the protective and provisional nature of God. He has provided a means of eternal protection for you through Christ. If he cares so much for your eternity, doesn't it follow that he would also care for your day-to-day issues? What is causing you to worry today? Identify those issues and consider what the Scriptures teach about trusting God in difficult times. Have you committed your life to Christ? If you're not sure, please read "Finding L.I.F.E. in Jesus" in the back of this book.

Faith in Action

Take some time to read a couple of additional texts from Scripture. They speak to God's promise of provision and protection in your life: Mt 6:25–34 and James 1:2–4, 4:13–17, 5:7–11; John 14:1–6. What do these verses teach about trusting God and his purpose and plan for our lives? What hope do they provide us for our future?

Prayer

Today as you pray, talk with God about the worries in your life. Be specific. Then, claim the truths that you read in the verses above. Finally, celebrate the gifts of grace that God has given you, including his promises of provision and protection.

Day 8

Our Prevailing God

Genesis 8:1–9:29

Standing on the seashore looking out at the ocean is an inspiring and intimidating sight. The deafening crash of the waves reveals an overwhelming, unharnessed power that could swallow me into its depths. The vast size of the ocean is equally daunting. At the edge of the horizon, at that place where the ocean and sky meet, huge ships appear as tiny specks. It's hard to imagine being out there alone in the middle of it all. That was Noah—just a small speck in the vast expanse of a suddenly formed worldwide ocean, tossed and carried upon the face of the frenzied waters.

The waters of Noah's flood were remarkable. The rain poured for forty days and nights (Gen 7:11–12). Apparently, there were powerful earthquakes that caused the water tables to erupt. It must have been dreadful. The waters of the heavens and the waters under the earth joined forces to form a worldwide ocean. The Bible describes these waters as "prevailing" on the earth.

The Bible says, "The waters prevailed and increased greatly on the earth. The waters prevailed so mightily on the earth that all the high mountains under the whole heaven were covered (7:18–19)." The waters prevailed so mightily that "all flesh died that moved on the earth (Gen 7:21)." And, "The waters prevailed on the earth 150 days

> *When we feel overwhelmed by the circumstances of life, we can rest in God's ability to prevail over anything.*

(Gen 7:24)." God had "blotted out every living thing that was on the face of the ground (Gen 7:23)." Those prevailing waters had generated a terrible power over the earth and all things that were on it. There was an exception, however.

In today's text, the mood of the flood story changes drastically. What had been a dreadful story of the near extinction of human life becomes a story of hope. It begins, "But God remembered Noah (Gen 8:1)." God didn't forget Noah and then suddenly remembered him. The phrasing is simply a rhetorical device to redirect our thinking from the unpleasant story of the flood to God's work in Noah's life. It's a positive way of saying, "God had not forgotten about Noah."

The ark had risen with the waters of the flood and now it rested upon the worldwide ocean (Gen 7:18b). Still, God had not forgotten that little speck of wood filled with the remnant of the earth's inhabitants. He was the one who had shut them up inside the ark, and he protected them through the prevailing flood. God had not forgotten. Then, God made the wind blow over the earth. The rain stopped, and the waters of the deep were plugged. "At the end of the 150 days the waters had abated (Gen 8:3)."

The author has done a masterful job of highlighting the reversal of the flood's affects. In chapter 7, the water prevailed over the earth, over the mountains, over all flesh, for 150 days. In chapter 8, however, we are told about God prevailing over the once prevailing water.

At the command of God, the waters no longer prevailed. Seven times in chapter 8 we are told that the powerful floodwater submitted to God's authority. In Genesis 8:1, "The waters subsided." In Genesis 8:3, "The waters receded." We read that the waters abated in Genesis 8:3b and 8:5. In Genesis 8:11 we read that the water abated, and twice we are told that the water dried up (Gen 8:7, 13). The

Day 8

prevailing waters could not prevail over God, because he is the great prevailing God.

Further, as if to make certain we do not miss it, the author was vigilant to show the complete reversal of the prevailing flood. "The waters receded from the earth continually (Gen 8:3)." The prevailing waters lacked endurance: "At the end of 150 days the waters abated (Gen 8:3b)." The waters no longer prevailed over the mountains: "The waters continued to abate . . . the tops of the mountains were seen (Gen 8:5)." And we are told in the opening verse, "But God remembered Noah and all the beasts and all the livestock that were with him in the ark (Gen 8:1)." God is a prevailing God!

As a result, when we feel overwhelmed by the circumstances of life, we can rest in God's ability to prevail over anything. God can prevail over personal problems, sicknesses, enemies, and even geo–political unrest. God has not forgotten us, and he can prevail over those things that seem to threaten us should it be his will. God is the prevailing God in whom we must trust.

Not only did God remember Noah during and after the flood, but also God remembered Noah and provided for his future. Following the flood, God commanded Noah and his family to produce offspring in order to replenish the earth (Gen 9:1, 7). God also established what we call the "food chain" (Gen 9:3) and established the basis of a justice system (Gen 9:6).

But most importantly, God established a covenant with Noah and his children after him (Gen 9:8–17). Following the harrowing time of the flood, God wanted Noah and his family to feel his protection. So, he offered a covenant to Noah and his family. In the ancient Near East, covenants were like the contracts of today. In those ancient covenants, two parties would establish the covenant guidelines, with both parties mak-

> *The Bible is full of promises that flow from God's gracious nature.*

> *God can prevail over our most difficult circumstances and provide for our spiritual, emotional, physical, and financial needs according to his gracious character and will.*

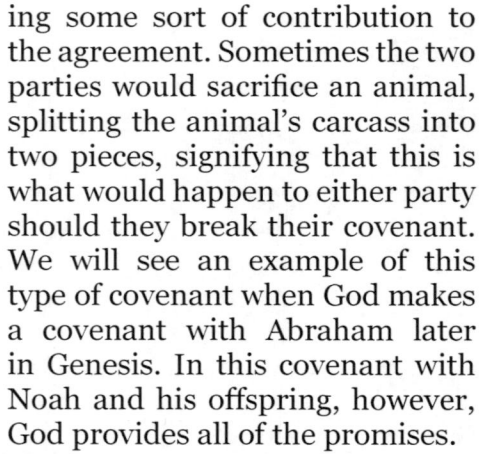

ing some sort of contribution to the agreement. Sometimes the two parties would sacrifice an animal, splitting the animal's carcass into two pieces, signifying that this is what would happen to either party should they break their covenant. We will see an example of this type of covenant when God makes a covenant with Abraham later in Genesis. In this covenant with Noah and his offspring, however, God provides all of the promises.

God even established the rainbow as his covenant sign. Every time Noah and his offspring saw the rainbow they would recall that God prevailed over the waters and would provide protection for them in the future. God would never again cause such a catastrophic flood; the rainbow was the covenant reminder of it. The promise of God began with Noah and extended to all of humanity.

We, too, are recipients of God's providing nature. The Bible is full of promises that flow from God's gracious nature. The apostle Paul told the Philippian church about God's provision: "And my God will supply every need of yours according to his riches in glory in Christ Jesus (Phil 4:19)." God can prevail over our most difficult circumstances and provide for our spiritual, emotional, physical, and financial needs according to his gracious character and will.

God has offered a covenant to us through Jesus' death and resurrection. At the last supper Jesus said, "This cup that is poured out for you is the new covenant in my blood (Lk 22:20)." You see? God provided a new covenant through Jesus. We enter into that covenant when we place our faith in him. When the Holy Spirit seals the covenant by his presence in our lives, we receive God's promises of forgiveness, adoption into his family, and eternal life.

Day 8

Just like God prevailed over the flood and provided for Noah, so he prevails for us today. If you ever feel like that little speck of an ark on the floodwaters of a turbulent life, trust in the God who prevails over everything. He will not forget you. When you have needs that are greater than you can meet, trust in the God who provides. He will provide for you. If have not entered into that faith covenant with God through faith in Jesus, believe in Him today for eternal life.

Food for Thought

What circumstances are you facing in your life today? Are you struggling with personal issues, family struggles, or financial problems? Are you or someone you love experiencing an extended illness? Or, are you struggling with whether you're a Christian? If God can prevail over extreme circumstances like Noah's, don't you think he can prevail over your circumstances too?

Faith in Action

Challenging circumstances are often accompanied by worry. However, Jesus said that worry wouldn't do a thing to change your circumstances (Mt 6:27). Today, you may be tempted to worry. When you feel that fear, choose to pray instead. Talk with God and trust him to work in your life.

Prayer

In today's prayer time, spend time talking with God about the challenging circumstances in your life. While it's true that God knows what's going on in your life, there is great value in casting your cares before him, because he cares for you. Give them to God and trust him to provide for your life.

Day 9

God Loves Us

Genesis 10:1–32

"Blah, blah, blah." Have you ever said that? This well-worn phrase is used either to skip over meaningless dialogue or to imply sarcastically, "Yeah, yeah, yeah, I've heard enough already." Sometimes when we're reading Scripture we do a similar thing. This is especially true when we come to passages like Genesis 10. When we get to verses like, "Cush fathered Nimrod (Gen10:8)," or "the territory of the Canaanites extended from Sidon in the direction of Gerar (Gen 10:19)," we tend to tune it out, and basically say, "Blah, blah, blah."

We can actually learn a great deal from reading through these passages, however. Obviously, those who love genealogy and family trees will find themselves drawn to such passages. There are other things that we can glean from these "blah, blah, blah" passages too. Think about it. Since the Bible is God's inspired message to us, then even the most challenging passages are intended to teach us something. We just need to spend enough time reading them and meditating on them to appreciate and understand their purposes.

The genealogy and territorial descriptions found in Genesis 10 teach us some important truths. First, we learn that God keeps his word. Sometimes God has bad news to share, like the news of the flood that he shared with Noah. God hates sin and always judges it. He always keeps his word.

> *God always keeps his word, and we receive the benefits of his promises.*

Sometimes, God has good news to share, like his promise to deliver Noah, his family, and the animals in the ark from the flood. God remembered Noah, and gave him the sign of the rainbow as evidence of his promises. Then, in Genesis 10:1 we are introduced to the generations of the sons of Noah. Again, God always keeps his word. He does that with us too. The Bible is filled with amazing promises of blessing, provision, guidance, protection, and salvation, just to name a few. God always keeps his word, and we receive the benefits of his promises.

Second, we learn that God loves the world. Genesis 10:5, 32 reveal that people eventually spread across all the lands of the earth. God loves the world and its inhabitants, and he wants his creation to prosper and thrive. In our previous readings we learned how God had appointed the rainbow as the sign of his promise to never destroy the earth with water again. God loves all of his creation.

Third, we learn that God is patient with his people. Perhaps we focus too much on the harsh judgment passages of the Bible because they frighten us. But God displays great patience with humanity long before he sends judgment. Think about it—God could have destroyed all of humanity; it was his right. He had created the earth from nothing, and he could certainly do it again. Instead, God showed patience and grace to Noah by saving his family from the judgment of the flood.

You might be wondering about the people who perished. What about them? The Bible never tells us exactly how long it took Noah and his sons to build the ark. But obviously, it took a long time for Noah and his sons to build such a huge vessel by themselves. During that time, we can be pretty certain that Noah told people what he was doing. Word would have spread, and everyone would have heard about Noah's construction project. Yet, none but Noah's

Day 9

family came into the ark. God gave time for people to respond to the news of the coming flood with repentance, but without effect. God was patient, even though the people rejected his message.

Consider the words of the apostle Peter. He wrote, "They formerly did not obey, when God's patience waited in the days of Noah, while the ark was being prepared, in which a few, that is, eight persons, were brought safely through water (1 Pet 3:20)." God was patient with sinners in the days of Noah.

What do these principles mean for us? They remind us that God still loves the world and the people in it. The apostle Paul wrote, "God shows his love for us in that while we were still sinners, Christ died for us (Rom 5:8)." The apostle John concurred, "See what kind of love the Father has given to us, that we should be called the children of God (1 Jn 3:1)."

Also, we are reminded that God will demonstrate a measure of patience toward us, too. The apostle Peter knew about God's patience. Three times he denied Jesus; he even denied knowing Him (Mt 26:69–75). But Jesus was patient with him. John wrote that Jesus came to see the disciples on the shores of Galilee after his resurrection (Jn 21:15–17). Three times Jesus asked Peter if he loved him. Three times Peter affirmed his love for the Lord. Each time Jesus told him to feed his people. This appears to be an undoing of Peter's three denials. Years later Peter wrote, "The Lord is not slow to fulfill his promise as some count slowness, but is patient toward you, not wishing that any should perish, but that all should reach repentance (2 Pet 3:9)" God is patient with us. God is not slow concerning his promise of judging unrepentant sinners, and he's not slow concerning his promise of grace and mercy to those who repent from their sins and place their faith in Jesus.

> *God still loves the world and the people in it.*

Food for Thought Think about the people to whom you show love and patience. What kind of people are they? If you're like me, they tend to be your family and friends. It's increasingly difficult to show love and patience to acquaintances or strangers. What about your enemies? Yet, that's exactly what we were to God when Jesus died for us; we were enemies of God (Rom 5:10). This truth makes it all the more amazing that God would show us both love and patience, both before we know him and after!

Faith in Action Today, you will have opportunities to show love and patience to the people around you, maybe even to your enemies (Mt 5:44). Remember, we have to show love and patience when people fail to live up to our expectations. So, when that happens, let God's love and patience show in your life. Your ability to demonstrate these attributes may be the very thing that points someone towards faith in Jesus.

Prayer

While you're praying today, spend time thanking God for the love and patience he has shown you through Christ. Also, rejoice in the fact that God always keeps his promises to you. Finally, ask God to help you show his love and patience to all of the people in your life today.

Day 10

Say What?

Genesis 11:1–9

At the time of this writing, the world's tallest building is the Burj Khalifa tower in Dubai, United Arab Emirates. Completed in 2010, it's 2,717 feet tall! The Empire State Building in New York City, completed in 1931, was once the tallest building in the world. In fact, it held that distinction for more than forty years. But its height of 1,454 feet pales in comparison to today's tallest buildings. Currently, there are more than twenty buildings worldwide that are taller than the Empire State Building. Someday one will be built that is taller than the Burj Khalifa. That is just the way humans naturally think: Bigger, better, taller.

Today's text reveals this long–held desire in the heart of man. In Genesis 11:4 we read, "Then they said, 'Come, let us build ourselves a city and a tower with its top in the heavens, and let us make a name for ourselves." God responded by saying, "This is only the beginning of what they will do. And nothing that they propose to do will now be impossible for them (Gen 11:6)." In response, God did an amazing and surprising thing—he confused their language and dispersed them over the face of all the earth. Consequently, the building project was scrapped (Gen 11:8–9).

It seems that the inclination of humanity after the fall was self–promotion and self–fulfillment. The builders of Babel wanted to be bigger, better, stronger, or taller; they wanted to make a name for themselves. Their desire

> *When people pursue self-promotion or recognition it places the focus on them rather than God.*

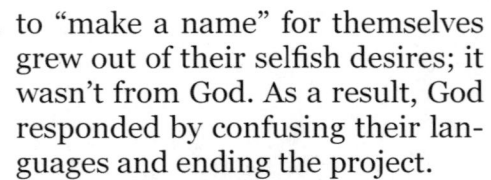

to "make a name" for themselves grew out of their selfish desires; it wasn't from God. As a result, God responded by confusing their languages and ending the project.

Such behavior was no surprise to God. After the fall of Adam and Eve, the Bible states, "The LORD saw that the wickedness of man was great in the earth, and that every intention of the thoughts of his heart was only evil continually (Gen 6:5)." This heart bent toward evil drove the tower builders in Babel to desire a name for themselves. The evil imagination of their hearts led them towards a selfish agenda. In this way, the Tower of Babel story points the reader back to the garden, where Eve and Adam made a selfish attempt to be like God (Gen 3:6–ff).

In our modern age, we have a practice of naming buildings after people. To be fair, often those buildings are named for worthy donors or philanthropists. However, some donors give monies expecting buildings to be named after them. It's a way of preserving their legacy, or worse, simply making a name for themselves.

Maybe that's why God reacted to the builders of Babel the way he did; when people pursue self–promotion or recognition it places the focus on them rather than God. Jesus said, "If anyone would come after me, let him deny himself and take up his cross daily and follow me. For whoever would save his life will lose it, but whoever loses his life for my sake will save it. For what does it profit a man if he gains the whole world and loses or forfeits himself (Lk 9:23–25)?" That's not to say that those who have buildings named after them are guilty of this sin. Ultimately, it's about the motives of their hearts. If the intent of their hearts

> *God wants people to focus on building his kingdom and legacy not their own.*

Day 10

is to make a name for themselves or to preserve their own personal legacy, their focus is wrong. God wants people to focus on building his kingdom and legacy not their own.

> *Any time we promote ourselves we are simultaneously demoting God.*

Perhaps there is another reason why God reacted so negatively to the builders of Babel. Not only were they promoting themselves, but also they were demoting him. In ancient Mesopotamian religious culture, it was not uncommon to build a city and a tower for a patron god. In fact, scholars have identified more than twenty such complexes in ancient Mesopotamia where the ancient city of Babel existed. Those religious complexes included various temple buildings, where people came to worship and sacrifice to their god. Those complexes also included a tower, called a ziggurat. The ziggurat resembled a pyramid, but had no inside space. For the ancient Mesopotamians, the ziggurats served as a stairway or ladder for their god to come down into the temple. Can you imagine? They were demoting the Creator of the universe to a being who actually needed a stairway to come down from the heavens.

God responded by saying, "This is only the beginning of what they will do. And nothing that they propose to do will now be impossible for them (Gen 11:6)." He recognized that left unchecked, they would never stop promoting themselves and demoting Him. The text concludes, "So the Lord dispersed them from there over the face of all the earth, and they left off building the city (Gen 11:8)."

The key principle for us to learn is that any time we promote ourselves we are simultaneously demoting God. Deuteronomy 4:39 warns us against that foolishness, "Lay it to your heart, that the Lord is God in heaven above and on the earth beneath; there is no other." Isaiah 45:18 states, "For thus says the Lord, who created the heavens

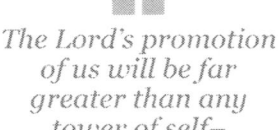

> *The Lord's promotion of us will be far greater than any tower of self-promotion we could build for ourselves.*

(he is God!), who formed the earth and made it . . . 'I am the LORD, and there is no other."

In the Gospels of Matthew and Luke, Jesus explained the concept like this: "No one can serve two masters, for either he will hate the one and love the other, or else he will be devoted to the one and despise the other (Mt 6:24; Lk 16:13)." When a person is devoted to self–promotion, God is demoted—we cannot serve two masters.

Satan even tempted Jesus to embrace a selfish agenda. After Jesus had been in the wilderness fasting for forty days "the devil took him to a very high mountain and showed him all the kingdoms of the world and their glory. And he said to him, 'All these I will give you, if you will fall down and worship me.' Then Jesus said to him, 'Be gone, Satan! For it is written, "You shall worship the Lord your God and him only shall you serve (Mt 4:8–10).'" Obviously, Jesus recognized the danger of abandoning the worship of God for the worship of Satan. He promptly and firmly resisted the temptation of the devil.

Remember, Satan's temptation, and the subsequent fall of Adam and Eve, revolved around self–promotion (Gen 3). In our culture, we're encouraged to embrace self–promotion too. But the Bible reveals that any time we promote ourselves we are simultaneously demoting God, by relegating Him to something far less than he is and wants to be in our lives. So, let's listen to what the brother of Jesus commanded us to do. James wrote, "Humble yourselves before the Lord, and he will exalt you (James 4:10)." The Lord's promotion of us will be far greater than any tower of self–promotion we could build for ourselves.

Day 10

Food for Thought

If you have received Jesus Christ as your Savior, you have also surrendered to him as your Lord. If we give him any place other in our lives than first place, we have promoted ourselves to lord of our lives and demoted him. Have you done this in any areas of your life? Is he Lord of your heart, your motives, your marriage and family, your job, your ministry at church, your hobbies, and your finances? If not, you're building your own Tower of Babel in your heart, and like those folks long ago, you will end up confused and scattered in your life.

Faith in Action

Examine yourself today. Check the motives behind what you're doing. Are you living for God's glory or your own? Identify the areas of your life that you haven't surrendered to God and make the conscious decision to yield those areas to the Lordship of Christ. We can only find what we truly desire by following Jesus (Mt 11:29–30).

Prayer

As you pray today, talk with God about your heart. If you've been living as the Lord of your life, building towers that promote yourself and demote God, confess those things to him and ask for his forgiveness. Then, submit to the Lordship of Christ in every area of your life today.

Day 11

Responding to God

Genesis 11:10–12:20

The other day I was watching television when my phone rang. The phone was in the other room, and I really didn't want to go get it. Then on the television, a message box appeared which read "unavailable" and listed an unknown number. So, I didn't go answer the phone. That's the really cool thing about our phone. Because our phone is connected to our satellite box, it allows me to hear the call, read the name of the caller, and make a choice about whether to answer it—all on my TV. Later that day the same event occurred. This time, however, the television message box said "Mom." Some calls demand an immediate response, so I jumped up and answered her call.

In Gen 12:1–9, Abram received a call from God that he chose to answer (remember, his name isn't changed to Abraham until Genesis 17). God called Abram to follow him and promised to make Abram a great nation, even giving the land of Canaan to his descendants. In today's text, Abram demonstrated the trust, response, sacrifice, and worship that became the standard for believers throughout the entire biblical text and continues to influence us today too.

With the conclusion of the Babel story, the reader of Genesis is guided through the Toledoth of Shem and then quickly on to the Toledoth of Terah (Gen 11:10, 27). The point of the Toledoth of Shem was to introduce Terah, and the point of the Toledoth of Terah was to introduce Abram,

30 Days to Genesis

> *God has spoken to us through creation.*

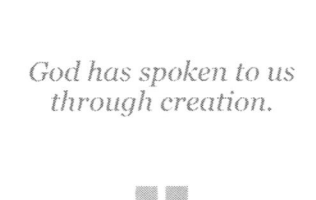

the character who dominates the stories found in Genesis 12–25. Abram was the son of Terah, and he was a descendant of Shem (Gen 11:26).

Terah and his family lived in Ur of the Chaldeans (Gen 11:27–28). The Chaldeans were the inhabitants of Mesopotamia, or Babylonia. Generally speaking, it's the region around modern day Iraq. In Genesis 11:31, we are told that Terah took his family, including Abram and his wife Sarai, toward the land of Canaan. We are not told why Terah wanted to move his family so far away. It could have been a famine or simply the desire to move.

Regardless, the ancient roads traversed through Mesopotamia, which means the land between the two rivers: the Euphrates and Tigris. The land just south of the Euphrates is hostile desert, while the land north of the Tigris is too mountainous for caravan travel. The primary route was between the rivers toward Canaan. For some reason the family stopped at the city of Haran. Haran was not Terah's initial destination, but they chose to settle there for a season, perhaps because Terah was ill (Gen 11:31). Terah died in Haran, naming Abram as the head of the family.

God spoke to Abram immediately following the death of Terah and called him into a covenant relationship that would shape the history of the world (Gen 12:1–3). We're not told how God spoke to Abram. The text simply says, "The Lord said to Abram (12:1)."

God has communicated with people since the beginning of creation. God and Adam spent time talking together in the Garden of Eden. God spoke with Noah and Abram. Similarly, God wants

> *God has spoken to us through his Son, Jesus.*

Day 11

us to know Him and desires a relationship with us. To accomplish this, God has communicated with people in three primary ways.

First, God has spoken to us through creation; we can look at all of the amazing things he's created and know that he exists (Rom 1:19). Second, God has spoken to us through his Son, Jesus. Hebrews 1:1–2 says, "Long ago, at many times and in many ways, God spoke to our fathers by the prophets, but in these last days he has spoken to us by his Son, whom he appointed the heir of all things, through whom also he created the world." Then, the writer of Hebrews heightens the truth spoken by Jesus when he writes, "Therefore we must pay much closer attention to what we have heard, lest we drift away from it. . . how shall we escape if we neglect such a great salvation (Heb 2:1–3a)?" Third, God has spoken to us through his Word, the Bible. Throughout the Bible we read phrases like, "Thus says the Lord." God used men to write the Bible so that we could know him. 2 Peter 1: 21 states, "For no prophecy was ever produced by the will of man, but men spoke from God as they were carried along by the Holy Spirit." As a result, "All Scripture is breathed out by God and profitable for teaching, for reproof, for correction, and for training in righteousness, that the man of God may be competent, equipped for every good work (2 Tim 3:16–17)." God has spoken in all of these ways so that we could both know about him and know how to have a relationship with him. As a result, our response to God's call is extremely important.

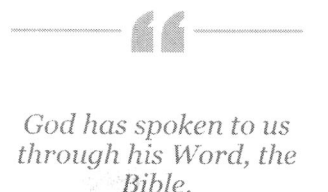

An immediate tension was created when God told Abram to leave his country and family in order to be blessed as the father of a great nation; his wife Sarai was barren. How can a man become the father of a great nation without the ability to have children? Abram was faced with a sudden crisis of faith. Could he believe the message of

> *God has spoken to us through his Word, the Bible.*

> *Faith is believing God's word and acting on it.*

God? Rather than doubt, however, Abram responded in faith.

In Genesis 12:4–6 we read that Abram chose to follow God. Notice all of the verbs in this text: Abram "went," "departed" (v.4), "took," "set–out," "came" (v.5), and "passed through" (v.6). The author wanted us to recognize that Abram did not sit still or settle down like his father, Terah. Abram's faith in God necessitated that he follow God—so he did.

In this narrative, Abram's faith is not hailed as something remarkable. God spoke, and Abram did what all of us should do when confronted with the call of God on our lives—he responded in faith. We might expect Abram to question God because he was childless, but he didn't. He went; he departed; he headed out. You get the point. God spoke and Abram responded. Here we discover the meaning of faith: faith is believing God's word and acting on it.

Once Abram believed and obeyed, God spoke to him in a more revealing way. "The Lord appeared to Abram (Gen 11:7)." In this appearance, God clarified the intent of his previous promise, "I will make you a great nation (Genesis 12:2)." God told Abram, "To your offspring I will give this land (Gen 12:7)." Once again God promised Abram a son, yet Sarai was still barren. How would Abram respond to this encounter?

Abram built an altar and worshipped the Lord. He acknowledged the greatness of God by offering a sacrifice. He believed that God could overcome Sarai's barren condition. Later, Abram built another altar and offered another sacrifice. Here, Abram did something new: he "called upon the name of the Lord (Gen 12:8)." Abram was worshiping his God, the one who could fulfill his promises, no matter how preposterous they might sound.

Day 11

Abram responded to God with faith, action, sacrifice, and worship. Each response by Abram revealed a deepening knowledge of God. Abram heard God speak, and he responded with simple faith. He didn't have all the answers, but he did trust in God. His faith motivated his actions. He set out to follow God wherever he might lead. As he followed God, God continued to reveal more of Himself to Abram, and Abram continued to respond with sacrifices of worship to God.

These verses in Genesis 12 have revealed the pattern of faith for followers of Christ. Jesus is the heart of God's communication to us. Our response should be one of faith and obedience. Faith will lead us to follow God by obeying his Word. As our faith matures and deepens, God will reveal more of Himself to us. As he does, our hearts will be captured by a love that produces both worship and sacrificial service.

Food for Thought

Isn't it great to know that God has chosen to speak to us? If he hadn't, it would be impossible for us to know about him or know him personally. Have ever considered the fact that the Bible is God's word for you? It contains "everything we need for life and godliness (2 Pet 1:3)." When you read the Bible, do you allow its truth to shape the way you live your life? God has given us this amazing book as a gift—let's make it the pursuit of our lives to both understand it and live it.

Faith in Action

The Bible tells us that it's impossible to please God without faith (Heb 11:6). Is God speaking to you through his word in some area of your life, but you're having trouble believing him? We can only please God when we believe and obey him. Today, consider how to begin obeying God in that area of your life.

Prayer

In today's prayer time, talk to God about any doubts you have related to his will for your life. Are you struggling with whether you can trust in God's promises? Talk with him about it. Then, commit yourself to obey and trust God's word and will.

Day 12

The Crucible of Faith

Genesis 12:9–14:24

In America, we have a court system based upon law. These laws promise protection to citizens and punishment for wrongdoers. A shared commitment to obeying the law is the foundation of any society. As citizens, we return again and again to the promises, protection, and prohibitions of the law. We act and rest in the promises of the law's guarantees.

In today's text, Abram experienced several important life events. These life experiences became the faith-building crucible through which he learned to trust God. Immediately following God's call and Abram's response in Genesis 12:1–8, God's promises appeared to be in doubt. Obviously, the weight of Sarai's barrenness was heavy on Abram's heart, but new threats arose from his neighbors. Abram made some poor decisions (Gen 12:9–20), Lot chose the best land in which to settle (Gen 13), and a coalition of local kings caused chaos which affected both Lot and Abram (Gen 14). Could God still make Abram a great nation in the midst of such turmoil and threats? As we will see, God always keeps his word, even overcoming our poor personal decisions and protecting us from decisions and chaos caused by others.

Genesis 12:9–20 demonstrates that God's promises are certain despite our poor decisions. After Abram began

> *Turning away from the promises of God is never a good decision.*

to call upon the Lord in worship, a severe famine came upon the land of Canaan (Gen 12:10). There is no time reference provided in the text, so we don't know how much time passed between Abram's worship experiences in verse eight and the threat of the famine in verse 10.

As the famine worsened, however, Abram turned away from the Promised Land and towards Egypt. Turning away from the promises of God is never a good decision.

Abram's poor decision to leave God's land was followed by an equally poor decision to tell the Egyptians that Sarai was his sister. This was a half–truth, because Sarai was only his half–sister (Gen 20:12). Abram feared for his life, thinking the Egyptians would kill him to take his beautiful wife Sarai for themselves. As a result, when the couple met the Egyptians, Abram told them that Sarai was his sister and didn't mention that she was his wife (Gen 12:12–13). Abram was correct in his assumptions. The Egyptians took Sarai, gave him some possessions in return, and spared his life (Gen 12:14–16). With Abram alone in a foreign land, and Sarai now a part of Pharaoh's harem, God's plan seemed very much in jeopardy.

God honored his promise, however, by striking Pharaoh's household with "great plagues (Gen 12:17)." The Hebrew word for plagues indicates skin conditions similar to leprosy. The Egyptians attributed this breakout to Sarai's arrival. At some point Pharoah questioned Sarai, and she confessed the scheme. We are told that Pharoah returned Sarai to Abram and asked, "What is this you have done to me? Why did you not tell me that she was your wife (12:18)?" While Abram's poor decisions appeared to put God's plans in jeopardy, God intervened to accomplish his promised plan.

Genesis 13 tells the story of Abram and Lot separating to keep peace in the family (v. 8–9). After the mis-

Day 12

takes of Egypt, Abram returned "to the place where he had made an altar at the first. And there Abram called upon the name of the LORD (Gen 13:4)." Abram acknowledged his bad decisions and returned to the place of blessing.

Abram's decision to repent and obey God might suggest that he would have no further troubles. After all, he had returned to the place of blessing and worship. In reality, however, walking with God does not eliminate life's hardships. It will, however, foster a trust in God that is bigger than those hardships.

God blessed Abram and Lot with such wealth in livestock that the land could not support both of their families (Gen 13:6). As a result, Abram proposed they split up. Graciously, he allowed Lot to choose the place where he wanted to move (Gen 13:8–9). Perhaps Abram's faith in God was maturing at this point. We're not told if Abram ever feared that Lot might choose Canaan, the land that God had promised him. Instead, we read that "Lot chose for himself all the Jordan Valley, and Lot journeyed east. Thus they separated from each other. Abram settled in the land of Canaan (Gen 13:11–12)." Lot chose what appeared to be the best land. The text describes it as a land as beautiful as the Garden of Eden (Gen 13:10). Though the choice seemed to favor Lot, time would reveal that it was a terrible decision.

After Lot made his choice, God renewed his promises to Abram. God reminded Abram that he would give all of the land of Canaan to his descendants. Afterwards, Abram settled near Hebron and "built an altar to the Lord (13:14–17)."

This event in the lives of Abram and Lot reminds us that God's promises are certain, and we should live with a steady faith in God. Even when others make decisions that affect us, God's

Walking with God does not eliminate life's hardships. It will, however, foster a trust in God that is bigger than those hardships.

67

> Trust and worship are direct results of knowing God and the certainty of his promises.

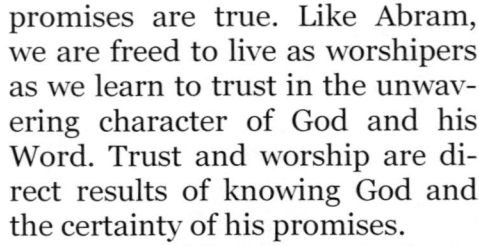

promises are true. Like Abram, we are freed to live as worshipers as we learn to trust in the unwavering character of God and his Word. Trust and worship are direct results of knowing God and the certainty of his promises.

In the following episode in Genesis 14, a coalition of kings banded together against the kings of Sodom, Gomorrah, Admah, and Zoar (v. 1–11). This was the region chosen by Lot. As the two factions warred, we're told, "They took Lot . . . and his possessions, and went their way (Gen 14:12). Lot was a captive. After hearing about Lot's situation, Abram armed the men in his household and pursued the Kings who captured Lot and his family. In a daring night raid, Abram's family army of 318 men attacked and defeated the marauders, rescuing Lot and all his possessions (Gen 14:13–16).

As they were returning home, Abram encountered a man named Melchizedek, who was a "priest of God Most High (Gen 14:18)." We shouldn't think of Melchizedek as a priest in the formal sense of those who served under the Law of Moses. Melchizedek, whose name means, "My king is righteous," was a man who was well–known for following and serving the Most High God. Unfortunately, there is little information about Melchizedek in the Bible; he is very mysterious. Interestingly, the author of the book of Hebrews uses Melchizedek as a type of Christ (Heb 7).

What we do know, however, is that Abram used this opportunity to worship God Most High. Somehow, Melchizedek recognized Abram's special relationship with God and pronounced God's blessing upon him (Gen 14:19–20)." Abram responded by giving a tithe of the spoils of war to Melchizedek as an act of worship to the God Most High; the one who had blessed him in battle.

Once again, the text has focused our attention on the certainty of God's promises. When we embrace and

Day 12

trust in God's promises, even in chaotic times, we are freed to trust and worship God. God's promises remain certain in uncertain circumstances.

Abram is rightly characterized as a man of incredible faith (Heb 11:8–19). His faith was not instantaneously strong and unwavering, however; it developed over time in the crucible of life's challenges. Those difficult circumstances both tested and strengthened his faith. Abram's faith was made great by experiencing the hardships of life and seeing God consistently delivered on his promises. Our faith will grow in the exact same way. We will learn to trust God and his Word in the midst of life's hardships. God is trustworthy and so are his promises.

> *When we embrace and trust in God's promises, even in chaotic times, we are freed to trust and worship God.*

Food for Thought — Our personal relationship with Christ does not shield us from the hardships of life— it equips us to navigate them for God's glory and the good of the gospel. The Bible reveals that our faith grows best when we encounter difficult circumstances (James 1:2–4). Why, you ask? Difficult circumstances force us to trust God and claim his promises. Are you in a difficult season of life? Pause to consider that God wants to use this time to build your faith as you rest in his promises!

Faith in Action — When you face difficult circumstances, you have only two possible responses: you can run towards God in faith or run from God in fear. Like Abram, fear will make us try and solve our problems on our own. Usually, this has bad outcomes. Faith, on the other hand, demands that we trust in God's promises and will for our lives. If you're struggling to live by faith today, consider calling your pastor or a strong Christian friend for encouragement and prayer.

Prayer — As you pray today, ask God to build your faith in his promises. After all, he has promised to meet your needs. If you're struggling with fear, talk with God about it. Claim his promise that "perfect love casts out fear." Ask God to remove your fears and replace them with faith.

Day 13

How to Mess–up the Plan of God

Genesis 15:1–16:16

My wife loves to tell a story about the time I attempted to repair the plumbing on our kitchen sink. I had never studied plumbing, never worked for a plumber, and never repaired a sink. But I was convinced I could do it; after all, I'm a guy. I mean, how hard could it be? Unscrew some rings, cut some pipes, put some new pipes in and glue—done! So, I didn't bother to call anyone or buy a book about plumbing; I just started working on the job.

I reached under the sink and grabbed the old, rusted, leaky pipe. Immediately, my thumb went right through it. Aggravated, I grabbed the pipe again in a vain attempt to protect my fingers. This time, the entire plumbing assembly under the sink fell out. I mean all of it, from the wall to the sink. All the traps and pipes were in a heap. I had totally annihilated the kitchen plumbing system without even trying. In retrospect, my plumbing plan wasn't very good—all I did was make a mess.

Unlike us, God's plans are always perfect, yet we often find ways to mess them up. Thankfully, as we saw in yesterday's reading, God is gracious and can overcome our messes to fulfill his will. Today's text is going to teach us how to avoid the big messes in our lives.

In Genesis 15, God speaks to Abram again and explains his promises in greater detail. God promised Abram

> *We make a mess of our lives when we listen to the voice of anyone but God.*

a son (Gen 15:1–5). While he'd made this promise to Abram previously, something was different in Abram's heart this time. Perhaps he'd accepted God's promise in his head, but this time he believed it in his heart: he "believed the Lord, and God counted it to him as righteousness (Gen 15:6)." Abram's faith was growing exponentially at this point, but the growth process was still progressing.

God reminded Abram that the land in which he wandered would be his as a possession (Gen 15:7). When Abram questioned how he could be sure these things would happen, God made a covenant with him (Gen 15:8–21). The text states, "On that day the LORD made a covenant with Abram, saying, 'To your offspring I give this land, from the river of Egypt to the great river, the river Euphrates (Gen 15:18).'" God would bless Abram with a son and their covenant would be the guarantee of that blessing.

One problem remained, however. "Now Sarai, Abram's wife, had borne him no children (Gen 16:1a)." This threat to the promise of God had been hanging over their lives for years (Gen 11:30). How could Abram have an heir from God when his wife was barren and childless? At this point the story of Abram's life gets messy.

In Genesis 16:1 we learn two things; First, Sarai was still barren; second, "She had a female Egyptian servant whose name was Hagar." Out of nowhere, Sarai concocted a scheme whereby Abram would take Hagar as his wife, so that Sarai could have "children by her." Sadly, "Abram listened to the voice of Sarai (Gen 16:2)." Then the drama began. Hagar conceived a child from Abram and promptly "looked with contempt on her mistress (Gen 16:4)." This story reveals some ways that we can make a mess of our lives.

We make a mess of our lives when we listen to the voice of anyone but God. Abram and Sarai had good intentions. In fact, the marriage customs of the day allowed such an arrangement. Still, their family was filled with turmoil at the very moment that Abram had two wives. Hagar, their former servant, became arrogant when she conceived a child, something her mistress was unable to do. Sarai, Abram's favorite wife, was undoubtedly sensitive about her inability to give Abram a son. To say the situation was sticky is an understatement. Which leads us to the second trouble spot.

We make a mess of our lives when we refuse to take responsibility for our actions. When the contention between his wives reached epic levels, Abram made a decision that made the situation worse, if that was even possible. Instead of accepting responsibility for his actions and exercising headship in his family to reconcile his wives, Abram simply avoided the problem. He said to Sarai, "Your servant is in your power; do to her as you please (Gen 16:6)." Notice, Abram didn't even acknowledge that Hagar was now his wife; he still referred to her as his servant. In response, Sarai dealt so harshly with Hagar that she ran away.

Abram believed God's promise that he would have a son, but we never read that he asked God about his decision to take Hagar as his wife. Instead, he listened to Sarai and created a huge mess in his family. He followed the plan of someone other than God and avoided taking personal responsibility for the actions that accompanied his poor decision.

This behavior is reminiscent of Adam's actions in the Garden of Eden. Adam abandoned his headship and listened to Eve and the urging of the serpent rather than God. Furthermore, once the mess was made, Adam avoided his responsibility for the sin by blaming Eve, "The woman whom you gave to be with me, she gave me fruit of the tree, and I ate (Gen 3:12)." Both

> *We make a mess of our lives when we refuse to take responsibility for our actions.*

> *We don't cultivate a deep faith overnight; it requires intentionality over time.*

Adam and Abram made a mess of God's plans by listening to other voices and avoiding responsibility for their choices. In both cases, their poor decisions plagued them all the days of their lives. The good news is that God acted to clean up the mess in both cases (Gen 16:7–16). Still, Adam and Abram had to live through the mess they created. Ismael, Abram's son through Hagar, was born when Abram was eighty-six years old (Gen 16:16). Ultimately, Abram had to deal with the conflicts between his two family units for another 89 years, until his death at 175 years old (Gen 25:7). We can learn several truths from Abram's poor decision about Hagar.

First, we must listen to God's voice above all of the competing voices in our lives and follow his plan above all other potential plans. Our contemporary world offers many life options, but God wants us to know and follow his plans for us. Jeremiah wrote, "For I know the plans I have for you, declares the LORD, plans for welfare and not for evil, to give you a future and a hope (Jer 29:11)." We may still mess up as we attempt to walk with God and accomplish his plan for our lives. After all, we're not perfect. David, the famous King of Israel, made some messes in his life, too. Yet, he reminds us that God is in control. He wrote, "The steps of a man are established by the Lord, when he delights in his way; though he fall, he shall not be cast headlong, for the Lord upholds his hand (Ps 37:23–24)." Life is hard enough without creating more hardship through foolish choices.

Second, we must take personal responsibility for our actions, both good and bad. God wants us to listen to his voice and follow his plan. If we do mess up, we should own up to it rather than ignore it. Difficult situations get worse, not better, when we refuse to take responsibility for our decisions, or worse yet, attempt to shift blame for

Day 13

them onto others. Two wrongs never make a right. Fortunately, the apostle John told us the way to proceed when we sin. He wrote, "If we say we have no sin, we deceive ourselves, and the truth is not in us. If we confess our sins, he is faithful and just to forgive us our sins and to cleanse us from all unrighteousness (1 Jn 1:8–9)."

Third, we must learn to trust God and his plans for our lives. The overarching lesson of the Abram narrative in Genesis, is his growth from one who doubts God to one who has deep faith in God. Between Genesis chapters 12 and 22, Abram's faith will develop from doubting God during a famine to the point of trusting God to raise his son from the dead, if necessary. We don't cultivate a deep faith overnight; it requires intentionality over time. Yet, it's the goal to which we aspire and the ultimate preventive against making a mess of God's plans for our lives.

30 Days to Genesis

Food for Thought — *Think back over your life. Can you remember a time when you took the advice of someone besides God and made a mess in your life? What was the outcome of that poor decision? Are you still dealing with those consequences in some way? How does today's study of Abram compare to what you experienced? Have you since owned that choice and taken responsibility for the consequences? The first step to making good choices is understanding the reasons behind your poor ones.*

Faith in Action — *Today, read Psalm 119:1–8 and reflect on these verses. What do they teach you about the value of knowing God's word? How does embracing God's plans for our lives protect us from making messes in our lives. When you make decisions today, especially if you have to make some big ones, pause to consider what God's word would say about those choices.*

Prayer — *As you pray today, spend some time talking with God about the lessons you've learned from today's study. If you're facing some big decisions, ask God for wisdom to understand what his word has to say about them. And, commit your plans to the Lord today. Ask God to guide your steps and help you fulfill his plan for your life.*

Day 14

The Friend of God

Genesis 17:1–20:18

In today's social media society, true friendship has been diminished. For instance, I have over 700 "friends" on one popular, social media site. Plus, the "people you may know" suggestions from that site make me aware of how many additional "friendships" I could have. I'm more perplexed, however, by how little I really know about many of my 700 social friends. Of course, I know who they are, and I've had interactions with them. I've actually met most of them, and I like them. For the most part they are family and acquaintances that I honestly like. To call them all "friends," however, is probably a stretch.

True friends are hard to find. There are probably 10–15 men in my life that I can go to any time, day or night, and they would stop what they're doing to talk with me or help me. They're true friends. Of those 15, there are five that I talk to on a regular basis, and even if we haven't talked in a while, it still seems like we just spoke yesterday. I laugh with these guys, share things in common with these guys, and reveal the true me. They understand my quirks, and I understand theirs. We accept one another for who we are; those are my best friends.

Abram is the only person in Scripture who is called a friend of God (2 Chron 20:7; James 2:23). Observing how Abram interacted with God will help us understand the actions of a friend of God. In turn, that should help build and strengthen our own personal friendship with God.

> *Abram's given name meant "exalted father," but his new name meant "father of a multitude."*

Thirteen years passed between the birth of Ismael and the beginning of Genesis 17. When Ismael turned 13, God re-affirmed his covenant with Abram and did two fascinating things. First, God changed his name to Abraham, "Behold, my covenant is with you, and you shall be the father of a multitude of nations. No longer shall your name be called Abram, but your name shall be Abraham, for I have made you the father of a multitude of nations (Gen 17:4–5)." Abram's given name meant "exalted father," but his new name meant "father of a multitude." From that day to this, the world has known Abram as Abraham.

Second, God declared that circumcision would be the sign of their covenant agreement (Gen 17:10). The physical act of circumcision created in Abraham and his descendants a physical distinction between the people of God and the surrounding nations. This physical distinction was meant to serve as an outward representation of the spiritual distinction of the people's covenant relationship with God.

During this renewal of their covenant, however, Abraham revealed a lack of trust in God. His problem wasn't with the act of circumcision; his problem was the fact that he still didn't have a son. Once again, God promised that Sarai would bear a child. This time, Abram scoffed and laughed, "Shall Sarai, who is ninety years, bear a child (Gen 17:15– 17)?" Clearly, Abram was struggling to fully trust God.

It's interesting to note at this point that when God re-affirmed his covenant with Abraham, it had implications for Sarai, too. First, God changed her name also. "And God a said to Abraham, 'As for Sarai your wife, you shall not call her name Sarai, but Sarah shall be her name. I will bless her, and moreover, I will give you a son by her. I will bless her, and she shall become nations; kings of

Day 14

peoples shall come from her (Gen 17:15–16).'" God's covenant wasn't just with Abraham; it included Sarah as well. Sarai's given name meant "princess," but her new name meant "noblewoman," a name befitting of the woman who would be the mother of a new nation of people related to God through covenant.

Second, God re-affirmed his plan to give them a son, even in their old age. God even told them what to name him: he would be called Isaac, which meant, "to laugh." Comically, God provided Abraham with a constant reminder of his propensity for disbelief (Gen 17:19); every time Abraham would say his son's name, he would be reminded of the time he laughed at God's promises.

Some time later, Abraham was visited by God to discuss the sins of Sodom and Gomorrah (Gen 18–19). While Abraham was learning to trust God in all things, he would have to watch from the sidelines as God destroyed the cities of the valley, including Sodom and Gomorrah. This would be especially difficult for Abraham, because Lot and his family lived there (Gen 13:10). Abraham negotiated fervently with God to spare the cities, but God destroyed them because there weren't five God-fearers in the whole region, including Lot's wife (Gen 19:26). Lot and his daughters were spared, but the influence of Sodom ran deep in their hearts; Lot was soon embroiled in a shameful, incestuous relationship orchestrated by his daughters (Gen 19:30–38).

We would think Abraham would have learned to trust God in anything, having experienced God's favor through all of these events; that was not the case. Genesis 20 reveals another event in Abraham's life where he encountered danger, and in order to save his own life, he defaulted to the lie that Sarah was his sister. Obviously, Abraham still had doubts about God's ability to protect him and provide

> *Sarai's given name meant "princess," but her new name meant "noblewoman."*

> *A friend of God will obey God's will even if it doesn't make sense.*

for him, despite their repeated covenant renewals. Abraham's friendship with God had many ups and downs. In those, however, I think there are several lessons we can learn about being a friend of God.

First, a friend of God will obey God's will even if it doesn't make sense (Gen 17:1–27). When God told Abraham that Sarah was going to have a child, he laughed. Can you imagine snickering in the face of the almighty? Me either! But, that's exactly what Abram did. The idea was so preposterous to him that he laughed at the thought of it. We have the benefit of hindsight, so we already know how the story ends. Still, Abraham did the hard part: he followed through with the covenant sign of circumcision (Gen 17:23–27). That was a huge step of faith. Even though God's plan seemed hilarious and ridiculous, Abraham obeyed God. A friend of God obeys God, even when his will seems absurd.

Second, a friend of God will draw near to God. As you recall, God and two of his angels visited Abraham and Sarah prior to the destruction of Sodom and Gomorrah. When the angels left to examine the cities of the plain, "Abraham still stood before the LORD. Then Abraham drew near (Gen 18:1–23a)." Abraham recognized God's authority in the situation. He drew near to God, approaching to talk with him as a friend.

Third, a friend of God walks with God in humility. God is never threatened by our questions; he doesn't turn away those who ask with a right spirit and attitude. In fact, James writes, "If any of you lacks wisdom, let him ask God, who gives generously to all without reproach, and it will be given him (James 1:5)." The problem is never the question—it's the attitude. Abraham

> *A friend of God will draw near to God.*

Day 14

stood still before the Lord, approached him, and humbly asked God about his will.

During their conversation, Abraham interceded diligently for his family. After all, he loved Lot and his family, and they were in danger if God was going to destroy the cities of the valley. Abraham begged God to spare the cities for the sake of the righteous people who might be living there. Finally, God said, "For the sake of ten [righteous] I will not destroy it (Gen 18:25–32)." The friend of God had interceded for his family; surely there were 10 righteous people in the valley. Sadly, that was not the case.

> *A friend of God walks with God in humility.*

Fourth, a friend of God will accept God's decisions. Once God declared his position, Abraham returned home. His intercession ended abruptly; he had accepted God's decision. Then we read, "Abraham went early in the morning to the place where he had stood before the LORD. And he looked down toward Sodom and Gomorrah and toward all the land of the valley, and he looked and, behold, the smoke of the land went up like the smoke of a furnace (19:27–28)." Abraham didn't question God any further; he trusted God.

Thankfully, God remembers his friends—those who trust in him. The text states, "So it was that, when God destroyed the cities of the valley, God remembered Abraham and sent Lot out of the midst of the overthrow (Gen 19:29)." God spared Lot because of Abraham, his friend.

> *A friend of God will accept God's decisions.*

Fifth, a friend of God may struggle with doubt at times. In Genesis 20, Abraham again doubted God's promise to protect him, so he lied about his true relationship with Sarah. Although God had proven repeatedly that he was faithful, Abraham still doubted

> *Each time we respond in faith, our level of trust grows stronger, and our friendship with God grows closer.*

him in a critical moment. Lest we think badly of Abraham, however, we should remember an episode from the life of John the Baptist. When he was imprisoned, John began to doubt that Jesus was the Messiah. After all, would the Messiah let him languish in prison? He sent some of his followers to question Jesus about it, even though he had heard the voice of God and seen the Holy Spirit descend upon Jesus at his baptism. Doubt is powerful, and at times it can overwhelm even those who are friends of God.

Abraham's faith journey should encourage us today. Each episode in our lives provides us with the opportunity to develop and express our faith in God. Each time we respond in faith, our level of trust grows stronger, and our friendship with God grows closer.

Day 14

> **Food for Thought**
>
> 1 John 3:1 says, "See what kind of love the Father has given to us, that we should be called children of God; and so we are."
> Further, he encourages us to call to him in the most familiar of ways: "You have received the Spirit of adoption as sons, by whom we cry, 'Abba, Father (Rom 8:15).'" This language expresses that we can come to the father as friends, yet we must do so in humility, surrender, and faith, always trusting that God's plans are best for us (Rom 12:1–2).

> **Faith in Action**
>
> Are you struggling with doubt today? Are you tempted to ignore God's will because it seems absurd to you? Have you come to believe that God's promises aren't for you? The principles and promises in God's word reveal his will and purpose for our lives. Believing and obeying God always leads to blessing, while disbelief and disobedience always leads to discipline (Heb 12:5–13). If you're tempted to doubt God today, remember these verses: "Trust in the LORD with all your heart, and do not lean on your own understanding. In all your ways acknowledge him, and he will make straight your paths (Pr 3:5–6)."

> **Prayer**
>
> When you pray today, ask God to reveal any areas in your heart where doubt resides. Name those areas specifically and confess your sin of doubt. Ask God to strengthen your faith in his promises and will and your desire to walk in obedience, even when God's plan doesn't make sense to you.

Day 15

The Day Laughter Came to Abraham and Sarah

Genesis 21:1–34

I come from a family of laughers. My earliest memories revolve around the times when our large family gathered at my grandparent's house. Everyone would laugh and laugh. Laughter was an adhesive that helped hold us together through tough times. Perhaps that is what author Laura Ingalls Wilder was describing when she said, "A good laugh overcomes more difficulties and dissipates more dark clouds than any other one thing." That was certainly the case for Abraham and Sarah, whose love story had been overshadowed by the dark cloud of barrenness.

Today's reading is about the day that laughter came to visit Abraham and Sarah. Laughter removed their gloomy clouds of emptiness. Laughter arrived in the home of Abraham and Sarah, bringing joy, happiness, and fulfillment for the remainder of their lives.

As you recall, Abraham and Sarah actually laughed at God's promise to give them a son. God had said to Abraham, "As for Sarai your wife . . . I will bless her, and moreover, I will give you a son by her. I will bless her, and she shall become nations; kings of peoples shall come from her (Gen 17:15–16)." Abraham's reaction is hilarious. The

> *We must remain obedient to God when blessings come into our lives.*

text says, "Then Abraham fell on his face and laughed and said to himself, "Shall a child be born to a man who is a hundred years old? Shall Sarah, who is ninety years old, bear a child (Gen 17:17)?" Abraham laughed in the face of the Almighty!

God continued, "No, but Sarah your wife shall bear you a son, and you shall call his name Isaac. I will establish my covenant with him as an everlasting covenant for his offspring after him (Gen 17:19)." In English, we miss the fact that Isaac literally means "to laugh, or he laughs." Laughter was on the way to Abraham's house.

Not only did Abraham laugh at the possibility of having a child; Sarah did too. As God was revealing to Abraham his plans to destroy the cities on the plain, he said to Abraham, ""I will surely return to you about this time next year, and Sarah your wife shall have a son (Gen 18:10)." Sarah overheard the conversation and the text says that because they were old "Sarah laughed to herself, saying, 'After I am worn out, and my lord is old, shall I have pleasure (Gen 18:12)?'" God then asked Abraham a question that must have shaped his thinking for years to come. He asked, "Is anything too hard for the Lord (Gen 18:14)?" From that point forward, Abraham and Sarah anticipated and eagerly awaited the day Laughter, in the form of their son Isaac, would arrive at their house.

So, what can we learn from this humorous story? First, we learn that Laughter came when God kept his word. If we learn anything from reading the Bible, it's that things happen when God shows up! God kept his word to Sarah, "The Lord visited Sarah, as he had said (Gen 21:1)." Here, we discover that God's visitation caused removed Sarah's barrenness. God showed up, and now Sarah was going to have a son, just like he said. Laughter came to Sarah because God came to Sarah! Similarly, we can ex-

Day 15

perience the joy of God's presence, too. When God visits, there is joy, happiness, and laughter.

Second we learn that Laughter came because God accomplished his will as promised. So that we don't miss the point, the author wrote, "And the Lord did to Sarah as he had promised (Gen 21:1b)." Four times in four verses (21:1–4), and twice in the same verse (21:1), we're told that God did what he said he would do. Laughter came to Abraham and Sarah, because the Lord fulfilled his promise. This lesson applies to us as well. When God promises something in the Bible, we can count on it happening. When God promises blessing, blessing will come; when God promises protection, protection will come. Laughter comes to us, too, because the God keeps his promises!

Third, we learn that Laughter came on time (Gen 21:2). God's timing is always perfect. Ecclesiastes 3:1 says, "For everything there is a season, and a time for every matter under heaven." God has never been late, and he's never been early—he's always on time.

Paul told the Galatians that God sent Jesus at the perfect time as well. He wrote, "But when the fullness of time had come, God sent forth his Son, born of woman, born under the law, to redeem those who were under the law, so that we might receive adoption as sons (Gal 4:4–5)." Jesus arrived at the perfect time in human history; it was the "fullness of time." We can experience laughter, joy, and blessings of eternal redemption through Jesus because God's timing is always perfect.

It's great to see how Laughter came to the house of Abraham and Sarah. In the story, their son Isaac was a living picture of the blessings and promises of God. God has promised us blessings also, so we should learn some biblical principles for how to receive the blessings and promises of God when they come into our lives.

> *We shouldn't value God's blessings more than we value God himself. We must live in obedience, even in seasons of blessing.*

87

> *We must recall God's goodness when blessings come into our lives*

First, we must remain obedient to God when blessings come into our lives. When Isaac was born, the text says, "Abraham circumcised his son Isaac when he was eight days old, as God had commanded him (Gen 21:4)." Abraham was overjoyed at the arrival of his son. There were still the commands of the Lord to obey, however. Abraham obeyed God's command concerning circumcision. He could have become so consumed by God's blessings that he forgot to obey God's commands, but he didn't. This becomes a great lesson for those of us who are follow Christ. We shouldn't value God's blessings more than we value God himself. We must live in obedience, even in seasons of blessing.

Second, we must recall God's goodness when blessings come into our lives. Sarah remembered God's great works when Laughter came to her home. She said, "Who would have said to Abraham that Sarah would nurse children? Yet I have borne him a son in his old age (Gen 21:7)." Sarah was in awe of God's great work as she remembered and rehearsed God's goodness. There is an old hymn that encourages us in this way: "Count your blessings, name them one by one. Count your many blessings see what God has done." Recalling God's work in our lives will renew the laughter, joy, and blessings of the event.

Third, we must celebrate God's works when blessings come into our lives. The text says, "And the child grew and was weaned. And Abraham made a great feast on the day that Isaac was weaned (Gen 21:8)." Abraham and Sarah celebrated God's work in their lives. God had blessed them with Laughter, and they rejoiced in it. The psalmist captures such a moment well when he says, "He gives the barren

> *We must celebrate God's works when blessings come into our lives.*

Day 15

woman a home, making her the joyous mother of children. Praise the LORD (Ps 113:9)!"

We must celebrate the good works of God, too. Psalms 139:14 states, "I praise you, for I am fearfully and wonderfully made. Wonderful are your works; my soul knows it very well." Let's live as worshipers today, both recognizing and celebrating God's blessings in our lives!

Food for Thought

Have you ever thought about the fact that God wants you to have great joy in your life? Jesus said, "These things I have spoken to you, that my joy may be in you, and that your joy may be full (Jn 15:11)." Joy isn't the same thing as happiness, however. Happiness is a temporary emotion based upon circumstance. Joy, on the other hand, is a state of being that results from a contentment rooted in God's promises and provision.

Faith in Action

Make a list of the blessings, joys, benefits, and protection that God has brought into your life. How many can you name? God visits us in his blessings, and we should continually give him praise for them (Phil 4:4). Remember the joy and laughter that accompanied God's visits to you. Worship God and smile today.

Prayer

In your prayer time today, spend time thanking God for all of the joy and laughter that he has brought into your life. These are good gifts from God. Rehearse your list of blessings before the Lord and bask in the joy that fills your heart.

Day 16

Abraham Offers Isaac Back to God

Genesis 22:1–25:11

In his fascinating book *The Dream Giver*, Bruce Wilkinson tells the story of Ordinary and the Dream Giver. Ordinary had been given a big dream by the Dream Giver. The journey to reach that dream, however, was tumultuous and extraordinary. Ordinary finally reached his big dream. Then he had the following conversation with the Dream Giver.

> Ordinary, said the Dream Giver.
> "Yes," said Ordinary.
> Give me your Dream.
> "What do you mean?" Ordinary asked. "It's my Dream. You're the one who gave it to me."
> Yes. And now I'm asking you to give it back.
> Ordinary was shocked, but he didn't even have to think. "I can't," he told the Dream Giver. "And I won't (*The Dream Giver*, 45)."

After a long season of contemplation, however, Ordinary reached a conclusion, "He could please the Dream Giver and surrender his Dream. Or he could go against the Dream Giver's wishes and keep his Dream, but risk losing the Dream Giver's pleasure. The choice broke his heart (*The Dream Giver*, 46)."

30 Days to Genesis

Abraham must have felt like Ordinary. In today's reading, God asked Abraham to give Isaac back to him, even though he had waited 100 years to receive him. God said to Abraham, "Take your son, your only son Isaac, whom you love, and go to the land of Moriah, and offer him there as a burnt offering on one of the mountains of which I shall tell you (Gen 22:2)." What? God had promised Isaac to Abraham and Sarah. He was the one who brought Laughter into their home. Now Abraham was supposed to offer him back to God as a burnt offering? You've got to be kidding!

The text offers us a small bit of relief from the moral angst of the story with these words: "After these things God tested Abraham (Gen 22:1)." God was testing Abraham through this event, and this helps us understand God's intent behind the command. Still, the question remains, "Is Abraham really going to kill his only son, Isaac?"

We might imagine that this test would have shaken Abraham's faith to the core of his soul. God had asked him to offer his beloved son as a sacrifice. Like Ordinary in Wilkinson's tale, Abraham was at a weighty crossroad. He could please God and sacrifice Isaac, or he could go against God's wishes and keep Isaac, but risk losing God's pleasure by breaking the covenant. It would seem that the choice would have broken Abraham's heart, but if it did, the text doesn't tell us. We are simply told, "So Abraham rose early in the morning, saddled his donkey, and took two of his young men with him, and his son Isaac. And he cut the wood for the burnt offering and arose and went to the place of which God had told him (Gen 22:3)." It appears that Abraham was ready for the test. We learn several things about responding to God's commands through this story.

First, we learn that tests of faith build on previous preparation. Abraham was prepared for the test. By this time in Abraham's life he had experienced numerous faith building events. He had journeyed from his homeland in Ur to follow God toward the land of promise (Gen 11:31–

Day 16

32; 12:1–9). He had to trust God for his provision after a famine precipitated his fateful flight to Egypt (Gen 12:10–20). He learned to trust God for blessings when Lot chose the best land in which to settle (Gen 13:1–18). He trusted God for protection when he fought to rescue Lot from the marauding kings (Gen 14). He trusted God with the outcome of his impatient decision to take Hagar as a wife in order to bear a son (Gen 15–16). He learned to trust God through intercession, when God was about to destroy the cities on the plain (Gen 18–19). He learned that God keeps his promises when he delivered Laughter into their home (Gen 21). Abraham's past experiences prepared him to respond properly to his present test of faith (Rom 4:13–25).

Second, we learn that tests of faith demand a faith response (Gen 22:3–10). God gave Abraham a command, "Take your son (Gen 22:2)," and God expected Abraham to comply. A faith test demands a faith response, and Abraham obeyed in faith. The text reveals that Abraham took Isaac to the place that God told him to go, bound him, and "took the knife to slaughter his son (Gen 22:10)." Abraham had promised Isaac that God would "provide for himself the lamb for a burnt offering (Gen 22:8)." The New Testament book of Hebrews says this of the event, "By faith Abraham, when he was tested, offered up Isaac [because] he considered that God was able even to raise him from the dead (Heb. 11:17–19)." Abraham's past experience prepared him to respond in faith, and he did—in the most amazing way!

Third, we learn that God sees our response to tests of faith (Gen 22:11–14). God acknowledged Abraham's response by providing the lamb for the offering. He said to Abraham, "Do not lay your hand on the boy or do anything to him, for now I know that you fear God, seeing you have not withheld your son, your only son, from me. And Abraham lift-

> *God sees our response to tests of faith.*

> *God blesses our response to tests of faith.*

ed up his eyes and looked, and behold, behind him was a ram, caught in a thicket by his horns. And Abraham went and took the ram and offered it up as a burnt offering instead of his son (Gen 22:12–13)." Abraham passed the test. God saw Abraham's faith and provided the lamb as a substitute for Isaac. God always sees our faith responses and rewards them.

Fourth, we learn that God blesses our response to tests of faith. (Gen. 22:15–19). God responded to Abraham's faith by declaring, "I have sworn, declares the LORD, because you have done this and have not withheld your son, your only son, I will surely bless you, and I will surely multiply your offspring as the stars of heaven and as the sand that is on the seashore. And your offspring shall possess the gate of his enemies, and in your offspring shall all the nations of the earth be blessed, because you have obeyed my voice (Gen 22:16–18)." God blessed Abraham's faith response, and because of his faith, God would now use Abraham and his offspring to bless the whole world!

Before we conclude today, however, we must pause to reflect on the larger implications of this event in Abraham's life. This event is a beautiful type of the gospel, revealed through the sacrificial death of Jesus Christ for our sins. As sinners, we are under the wrath of God, cursed to death and eternal separation from God (Rom 3:23; 6:23a). Because of God's great love, however, Jesus Christ came to be our substitute sacrifice. He is the ram caught in the thicket; the one who was willing to take our place, pay our debt, and die our death (Rom 5:8). Because of his sacrifice, we can be saved from an eternity separated from God if we will receive his gift of forgiveness by faith (Rom 6:23b).

Day 16

Food for Thought *Is God testing your faith in this season of life? If so, how is he doing it? Is he testing your willingness to believe his promises? Is he testing your willingness to obey his Word? How are you responding to that test? Are you running from God in that area of your life, or are you running towards him, knowing that he will bless your obedience?*

Faith in Action

Identify the main area where God is testing your faith. Is it in your life, your family, or your job? Is he calling you to become more obedient in his church through serving, giving, and making disciples? Today is the day to begin following God in that area by faith. What steps do you need to take to accomplish this?

Prayer

When you pray today, I want you to talk with God about the test of faith in your life. Ask him to help you understand his will and the way he wants you to respond. If you're running from God in some way, confess that sin and turn from it. Commit to live your life by faith today for God's glory!

The Other Son Syndrome

Genesis 25:12–18

Have you ever felt like the third wheel on a bicycle, or the extra pieces of a toy you were putting together, or the third runner–up in a beauty pageant? I have too. I played football from the time I was a five until I graduated from high school. I love the game. Because of my size and speed (or lack of thereof!), I was a lineman. Not just any lineman, but a guard—an interior lineman. Guards are the players that nobody recognizes, except the parents. Think I'm exaggerating? Quickly, name five famous left guards. You probably can't name one, let alone any famous ones!

On our high school football team, we had a running back that was an All–State performer; he was outstanding. Then, we had some tough defensive players who were voted All Region and All County; these guys were really good, too. Then, like on any football team, there were several others who touched the ball and scored touchdowns. They got the cheers and people knew their names. Then, there were defensive players who tackled the opposing runners. They got great cheers for scooping up fumbles, intercepting passes, and stopping the opposing team. All of these players experienced the fame of the Friday Night Lights.

Finally, there were the linemen. Some call them "the big uglies." Among linemen, there was a hierarchy. The two tackles played on the end of the line and protect-

> *God loves us, and understanding his great love should always make us feel significant and valued.*

ed the edges, including the quarterback's blindside; tackles were invaluable. The center was in the middle of the line and got to touch the ball every play; he snapped the ball to the quarterback. Finally, there were the two guards, positioned between the tackles and the center. Hello, I'm a guard.

Through the encouragement of my parents, church, and community, I was able to play guard without my psyche being bruised too severely. Even as a young kid, I realized that without guards, runners couldn't run, quarterbacks couldn't throw, receivers couldn't catch, and protecting the blindside of the quarterback would be irrelevant, because his front side would be bombarded with angry, charging defenders. Ultimately, I learned to be content with being a guard.

Today's text focuses on Ishmael, Abraham's "other son." Throughout the Toledoth of Terah, Abraham was the primary focus, and the sub–plot revolved around Isaac, the son of promise. Then, there was Ismael, the "other son," who probably felt like the odd man out. Ishmael was born to Abraham by Hagar, the maidservant of Sarah. As you recall, the scheme was the brainchild of Sarah, because she knew about God's promise to Abraham. She just wanted to move that promise along quicker than God had planned.

Ishmael appears sporadically in the story of Abraham. About the time one forgets he exists, he reappears to remind us of his presence. Ismael is truly "the other son," and he is presented as such in the text. Being the other son doesn't have to be life crippling, however. Let's consider some of the positive aspects of Ishmael's life and contemplate how they apply to our own lives in those times when we feel like the other son. First, God loved Ishmael. God showed up to offer love, support, and blessing when Sarah and Abraham mistreated Ishmael and his mother. When Sarah mistreated Hagar because she had conceived,

Day 17

God spoke to Hagar saying, "I will surely multiply your offspring so that they cannot be numbered for multitude (Gen 16:10)."

In chapter 17, God reiterated his covenant with Abraham, explaining that the child of promise would come from Sarah. Yet, God didn't forget Ishmael. He said, "As for Ishmael . . . behold, I have blessed him and will make him fruitful and multiply him greatly. He shall father twelve princes, and I will make him into a great nation (Gen 17:20)." God loved Ishmael.

God loves us too! John has written, "See what kind of love the Father has given to us, that we should be called children of God (1 Jn 3:1)." Paul stated it like this, "But God shows his love for us in that while we were still sinners, Christ died for us (Rom 5:8)." We must avoid the temptation to wallow in self–pity when we feel like the other son. God loves us, and understanding his great love should always make us feel significant and valued.

Second, Abraham loved Ishmael, too. In chapter 17, after God told Abraham that Sarah would have a child, Abraham exclaimed, "Oh that Ishmael might live before you (Gen 17:18)!" Abraham realized that Sarah and he were old, and he really wanted Ishmael to be the seed of promise. God had other plans, of course, but Abraham's exclamation reveals his love for his "other" son.

Parents can understand most clearly Abraham's capacity to love more than one child. Parents love their children equally, regardless of the success they achieve. We love them because they're our children, not because they are inducted into some hall–of–fame. Abraham felt the same. It's interesting that Ishmael participated in the burial of his father (Gen 25:9). Abraham loved Ishmael, and Ishmael loved his father. For Ishmael, he would always be his father's first son, and

> *Knowing someone loves us brings comfort and produces confidence for life.*

> *We should stop fixating on what we're not and be grateful for all.*

knowing he had his father's love must have been very reassuring.

Knowing someone loves us brings comfort and produces confidence for life. We may not have parents who love us like Abraham loved Isaac and Ishmael. We may never achieve the fame and fortune that many do. But, all of us have people in our lives that love us. There are grandparents, parents, spouses, children, friends, fellow Christians, and many others. That love provides us with great feelings of significance.

Now, let's reverse that thought process. Could there be someone in your life who really needs to feel the significance of your love? You could be the key to helping others overcome their "other son" mentalities. We love others and others love us, all because God loved us first (1 Jn 4:9).

Third, the other son syndrome doesn't apply to every area of our lives. Our reading today reveals Ishmael's great heritage and lineage. He was the leader of a great clan. In that setting, he was not the other son Ismael—he was THE MAN. He had twelve sons who had villages and encampments all over the southern and eastern portion of Canaan. Ismael was a man blessed by God.
He was not the one chosen by God as the covenant seed, but in the other areas of his life, he was Ismael the husband, the father, the leader of nations. He was viewed as a great man, and he died as a famous man. The other son syndrome did not apply to all areas of his life.

We may feel like the other son at different times, but God has no other son's. Because of our faith in Jesus, we're all loved equally by God and equipped to bring him glory through our lives. God gives us spiritual gifts to accomplish this work in us. The apostle Paul compares our unique spiritual gifts to the parts of a human body (1 Cor 12). The leg is very important for the body's transportation, so even if the leg is not the head, the leg is supreme in

Day 17

the area of walking. Our takeaway is this: we should stop fixating on what we're *not* and be grateful for all of the things we *are* because of God's grace towards us.

Fourth, we must understand that the blessings of others do not diminish the scope of our own blessings. God's love, provisions, and blessings are limitless. When God blesses others, his capacity to bless us is not diminished in any way. There is no need to be jealous, feel slighted, or respond like the other son. We can rejoice in the blessings of others, because we will still receive all of the blessings that God has reserved for us. We would do well to remember what David wrote, "I give thanks to you, O Lord my God, with my whole heart, and I will glorify your name forever. For great is your steadfast love toward me (Ps 86:12–13)."

Food for Thought

Do you ever feel like you're the other son in your life? Where do you feel that way—in your family or on your job? Why do you feel that way? Does it seem like other people always get the best opportunities or relational benefits? If you're not careful, you'll expend so much energy wishing things were different that you never actually express gratitude for all of the things that God has done for you.

Faith in Action

List the people in your life who love you, including God. How do they help you feel valued? Now, think about someone that needs to know that you love them. How could you make them feel special today. Make the effort to encourage them today.

Prayer

As you pray, spend some time thanking God for the love he has shown you through Christ. Also, thank God for the people in your life who love you. Finally, spend some time asking God to help you see the people around you who need someone to show them God's love.

Day 18

Struggling for Position

Genesis 25:19–34

My two sons loved video games when they were young. Since I'm a big kid at heart, I loved to play along with them. In one of the games, we would choose fantasy characters and race around bizarre tracks. The fun part was that we could throw items at each other, wreaking all sorts of havoc. We were so competitive that it didn't matter if we wrecked one another, just as long as we came in first place. In make–believe video games such behavior can be tolerated; in real life, however, such behavior causes serious, real–life trouble.

The Toledoth of Isaac begins following the story of Ishmael. Although this Toledoth is the family story of Isaac, Jacob dominates the story as the primary character. After the death of Abraham, the promises of God were passed on to Isaac. God made it very clear to Abraham and Sarah that Isaac was the child he promised. In today's text, Isaac's wife Rebekah gave birth to twins, Esau and Jacob. We're faced with a question here: which of the twins would be the next "child of promise?" Normally, the firstborn son got the birthright and the largest share of inheritance. As a result, the expectation would be for the promise to be passed along to their oldest son Esau. But in a twist that upset the order of the day, God chose the youngest son Jacob to be the child of promise. As you might imagine,

> *God knows everything about us.*

God's choice led to some surprising and tumultuous events in the lives of the twin brothers.

The drama of the story is heightened even more when we find out that God's child of promise had some major character flaws. The name Jacob means "one who supplants" and "deceiver." Jacob would be plagued throughout his life by his propensity for deception. It would be decades before he developed into a man who would obey and trust God like his grandfather Abraham. Let's consider how Jacob's story unfolds.

Initially, we observe that God knew about Jacob's struggles before he was even born (Gen 25:19–24). Verse 21 states that Isaac "prayed to the Lord for his wife." The form of the verb indicates a pleading prayer because Rebekah, like Sarah before her, was barren. Eventually, God answered his prayer, but the process was a lengthy struggle; Isaac and Rebekah had been married for 20 years before their twins were born (Gen 25:26).

The text reveals that not only had Rebekah conceived, but also she had conceived twins. Without the benefit of modern medicine, she discovered she was carrying twins because of how they struggled in her womb. She was worried because of the amount of movement within her, so she sought the Lord for the answer. God revealed that she was carrying twins, and they would be born into unsettling circumstances.

God revealed that the twins would be two nations, and they would be divided from the time of their birth. One would be stronger, and the older would serve the younger. God told Rebekah about a major struggle that began in the womb and would continue after their deaths. God knew about the struggle of Jacob and Esau before they were even born.

Next, we observe that Jacob's struggles were foreshadowed at his birth (25:25–26). Esau was born first;

Day 18

he was a redheaded, hairy baby. In fact, his name means "hairy." The text seems to indicate that as Esau made his entrance into the world, Jacob was close behind. The text says that as Esau came out, Jacob was holding onto his heel. Even then, Jacob was struggling to supplant Esau as the firstborn, from the very moment of birth. Because of this, his parents named him Jacob, "The supplanter." Jacob was born into this world struggling for something that was not his; he was supplanting from the moment of his birth.

Finally, Jacob's struggles were evident as he approached adulthood (Gen 25:27–34). As Esau and Jacob grew into adults, they took different career paths. Esau was a hunter and the favorite son of his father Isaac, who loved to eat the wild game Esau harvested. Jacob was a chef and the favorite son of his mother Rebekah.

After a hunting trip, Esau returned home hungry to the point that he felt like he would die. Esau saw Jacob cooking some lentil stew and asked for some of the food. In a cunning move, Jacob offered to give the stew and bread to Esau, but there was one stipulation; one huge price to pay: Esau would have to trade his birthright for it. Esau felt so ravenously hungry that he "despised his birthright (Gen 25:34)." He traded his position as the firstborn for some lentil stew and bread. I suppose he thought what's the point of having a birthright if you die before you can enjoy it? Jacob had found a way to supplant Esau. God foretold it, it was foreshadowed in their birth, and it finally came to pass.

There are some lessons for us to learn here. First, God knows everything about us. God described Jacob and Esau's character traits while they were still in the womb. God knew they would have a great struggle. God reminded the prophet Jeremiah of the same thing when he was calling him to be a prophet. God said,

> *God sent Jesus to atone for our sins and to cover our sinful natures with the righteousness of Christ.*

> *God is patient with us, and he will mold us into useful vessels to accomplish his kingdom plans.*

"Before I formed you in the womb I knew you, and before you were born I consecrated you; I appointed you a prophet to the nations (Jer 1:5)." God knows our character from the moment of conception.

Second, we are born with a sin nature that accompanies us for life. Jacob's sinful character flaw was evident from the time of his birth, but that's the case with all humans. Remember, Adam's sin caused all of humanity to have a sin nature as well (Rom 5–7). That's why we sin—because we have a sin nature. God sent Jesus to atone for our sins and to cover our sinful natures with the righteousness of Christ.

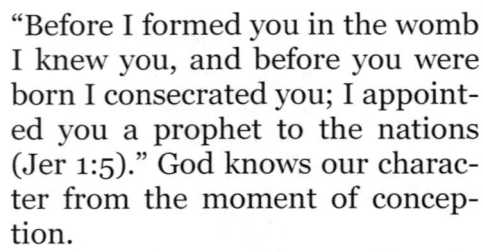

Third, God shapes and molds us into useful vessels of his promise. Jacob's deceitful nature would plague him his entire life, yet God succeeded in molding him into the father of the nation of Israel. God gave Jeremiah a vivid example of this molding process. God told him to go to the potter's house and "there I will let you hear my words (Jer 18:2)." Jeremiah saw that "the vessel he was making was spoiled in the potter's hand, and he reworked it into another vessel, as it seemed good to the potter to do (Jer 18:4)." Then God asked Jeremiah a question that remains pertinent for us today, "Can I not do with you as this potter has done? Behold like the clay in the potter's hand, so are you in my hand (Jer 18:6)."

God wants to ask us the same question. Can he shape and mold us into useful vessels? Yes. We can absolutely expect God to do the same for us today. The story of Jacob is one of hope--it reminds us that when God chooses us for his purpose, he begins transforming our character flaws. It reminds us that God is patient with us, and he will mold us into useful vessels to accomplish his kingdom plans!

Day 18

Food for Thought

Isn't it great to know that God knows everything about you and loves you anyway? It's also good to know that because God started the good work in us through Christ, he won't quit until it's completed (Phil 1:6). God doesn't work in a vacuum, though. We must be active participants in the process by seeking God's will through his Word, so that God can shape us as he wills.

Faith in Action

You've been working through this devotional for a little over two weeks now. As you've been reading, what areas of your life has the Holy Spirit been prompting you about? Write them down. What steps does God want you to take to cooperate with him in your growth in these areas?

Prayer

In your prayer time today, spend some time talking with God about the work he wants to do in your heart. If you've been resisting it or ignoring it, ask God to help you understand why. Commit to let God be the potter and shape your life as he wills; his plans are perfect.

Day 19

Jacob's Web

Genesis 26:1–27:46

My parents owned a large piece of land on top of a mountain, most of which was covered in woods. We spent a lot of time in those woods hunting or hiking as we grew up. Often, while walking through the woods, I would walk into a spider's web. I hated that, and I still do. I don't have arachnophobia, though. I hate the webs more than the spiders! When I'm entangled in a web it makes me feel like spiders are crawling all over me. I flail my arms and run in an attempt to escape those awful webs, spun by innocent spiders trying to catch a meal.

In our text today, we'll discover that Jacob had to flee from a web of deceit he spun himself. His deceiving and supplanting nature finally caught up with him, and he was forced run for his life. In Genesis 27, we're told how Jacob tricked his father Isaac into blessing him instead of Esau. Esau's angry response threatened Jacob's future as the promised son.

As the story resumes, Esau and Jacob are about forty years old. Esau has taken two wives from neighboring cultures, and it grieved his parents (Gen 26:34–35); Jacob had not yet married.

Isaac was getting old, and he knew he would soon face death. It was the custom of the day that the patriarch of the family would speak blessings, or curses, over his children before he died. The blessing of the father was irrevocable. It was a decree from the father concerning the future of the family and the family assets. Isaac was preparing to speak he blessings over his sons, and he wanted to give his firstborn son, Esau, the blessing of the firstborn.

If you recall, however, Esau had despised his birthright and sold it to Jacob for food (Gen 25:29–34). Isaac chose to ignore that, however. He knew that Jacob had cheated his son, and he wasn't about to let it change his mind about who deserved the inheritance of the firstborn. Isaac told Esau to go hunting and bring him a wild game meal, after which he would bless him (Gen 27:1–4). Rebekah was eavesdropping on Isaac, however, so after Esau left, she helped Jacob spin his deceitful web (Gen 25:28; 27:5–17).

To pull it off, Rebekah developed a plan to trick Isaac into believing that Jacob was Esau. The problem was that the twins were fraternal. Esau was hairy, and Jacob was smooth skinned (Gen 27:11); their voices were different too (Gen 27:22). In order to fool her husband, Rebekah told Jacob to get two young goats from the flock, and she would make Isaac a meal that tasted like wild game (Gen 27:9). She said, "Then you shall take it to your father, that he may eat it and that he may bless you before his death (Gen 27:10)."

Jacob thought he had already secured that blessing when he sold his stew to Esau for the birthright (Gen 25:29–34). While Isaac had no intentions of honoring that sale, God had declared that the oldest would serve the youngest (Gen 25:23). To make the ruse plausible, Rebekah put Esau's clothes on Jacob and put animal skins on his arms and neck (Gen 27:11–17). This would make Jacob smell and feel like his brother Esau. At this point, you may be wondering how this could possibly work? The answer is simple: Isaac was nearly blind in his old age.

When Jacob brought the food to his father, Isaac was surprised. How had his son harvested an animal and cooked it so quickly? Jacob lied and told his father that God had brought it to him (Gen 27:18–20). Still, Isaac had some uncertainty. He recognized the voice of Jacob, but

Day 19

he was fooled by the apparent smell and feel of Esau (Gen 27:23, 27). Ultimately, Rebekah's plan worked. We're told that Isaac "did not recognize him, because his hands were hairy like his brother Esau's hands. So he blessed him (Gen 27:23)." Jacob received the official blessing of the firstborn (Gen 27:27–29). Isaac's blessing stated that the family would "bow down" to him (27:29)." His birth position didn't warrant that privilege, but he had successfully supplanted Esau as the firstborn, and he had received the blessings that accompanied it.

Isaac and Esau were livid when they discovered the deception (Gen 27:30–34). Esau begged his father to bless him as well, but Isaac replied, "Behold, I have made him lord over you, and all his brothers I have given to him for servants, and with grain and wine I have sustained him. What then can I do for you, my son (Gen 27:37)?" Isaac gave Esau some hope, however. He said, "You shall serve your brother; but when you grow restless you shall break his yoke from your neck (Gen 27:40)."

Jacob' deceit helped him obtain the birthright and the accompanying blessings, but in the process, he was trapped in the web of his own deception. We're told, "Esau hated Jacob because of the blessing with which his father had blessed him, and Esau said to himself, 'The days of mourning for my father are approaching; then I will kill my brother Jacob (Gen 27:41).'"

When Rebekah and Jacob heard about Esau's threat, Jacob fled for his life and traveled to Haran, the land of his fathers (Gen 27:42–28:7). As you recall, God called Abraham from that land. Now, he would have to do the same with Jacob if his promises to Abraham were to be fulfilled. Sadly, Jacob's deceitful web would continue to entangle him until he yielded to God's will, an event still some twenty years in the future.

> *Jacob lied and spread discord in his family, and that is clearly against God's nature and will.*

> *Deceit always hurts other people.*

This episode of Jacob's story, with all its lies, deceit, and trickery, is befitting of a modern, TV soap opera. This raises a tough question, however. Was Jacob's deceiving and lying a part of God's plan? The answer is no. God chose Jacob to receive the promises of Abraham, but he didn't plan for Jacob to lie and deceive his way into the birthright; that would have been contrary to God's character. The ninth commandment God would give to Moses commands believers to tell the truth (Ex 20:16). Proverbs 6:16 affirms this, "There are six things that the LORD hates, seven that are an abomination to him." One of those seven things is "a false witness who breathes out lies, and one who sows discord among brothers (Pr 6:19)." Jacob lied and spread discord in his family, and that is clearly against God's nature and will.

Proverbs 20:21 adds, "An inheritance gained hastily in the beginning will not be blessed in the end." God wanted to bless Jacob with the blessings of Abraham—he didn't need the help of Jacob's lies and deceit. God wasn't the cause of Jacob's deceit; Jacob was and his actions were sinful.

This event in Jacob's life teaches us an important principle: deceit hurts people. Esau was hurt, and his hurt tuned to anger. His anger turned to hate, and his hate to thoughts of murder. Isaac was hurt also. When he learned that he'd been deceived by Jacob, he became so distraught that he trembled and shook (Gen 27:33). Rebekah was hurt, too. Jacob was her favorite son—he was a momma's boy. She had to send her favorite son away to protect his life (Gen 27:42–28:5). Deceit always hurts other people.

Not only will deceit hurt others, but also it will hurt the deceiver. Ultimately, the deceiver will get caught up in his or her own web of deceit. The lies simply become too

Day 19

difficult to sustain. Jacob hurt the people around him, but he was hurt as well.

Sure, Jacob got what he'd wanted since birth. He tried to exit the womb first, grabbing Esau's heel. He traded food for Esau's birthright. Finally, he tricked his father into blessing him as the firstborn son. Jacob got what he had wanted, but what good was it to him in the end? Jacob's birthright had no practical benefits, because he was an outcast in Haran, hundreds of miles from his family. What good is it to be a leader of the family when you're not near them? Sadly, Jacob was trapped in his own web of deceit.

> *Jacob hurt the people around him, but he was hurt as well.*

30 Days to Genesis

Food for Thought

Have you ever been caught up in a web of deceit? Was it a web of your own making or of someone else? How did it affect your life? If not, have you had some friends who got trapped in deceit? What lessons can you learn for your own life about the dangers of deceit? If you're trapped by lies and deceit, contact someone you trust today and ask for help.

Faith in Action

Everyday we are confronted with situations that test our commitment to truth. It's easy to succumb to the temptation to tell the little, white lie. Yet, lying always requires deceit at some level. Choose truth today.

Prayer

As you spend time with God in prayer today, talk with him about the importance and value of truth. It's one of God's character traits, and he wants to see it in you. If your struggling with lies and deceit, confess them to God today.

Day 20

Jacob's Harvest and God's Surprise

Genesis 28:1–31:55

My wife and I enjoy planting our raised–bed vegetable garden. It isn't very large, but it's fun to plant seeds and eat the harvest. The thought occurred to me that the planting process and the anticipation of the harvest involved simple principles. If you plant a bean seed, you'll get a bean plant that produces lots of other beans. Plant tomato seeds, and you'll get tomato plants that produce lots of tomatoes. Plant squash seeds, and you'll get a squash plants that produce lots of squash. You get the idea. It's the law of sowing and reaping—you reap what you sow.

The Bible has applied the principle of sowing and reaping to life. The apostle Paul wrote, "Do not be deceived: God is not mocked, for whatever one sows, that will he also reap. For the one who sows to his own flesh will from the flesh reap corruption, but the one who sows to the Spirit will from the Spirit reap eternal life. (Gal 6:7–8)." Beans produce beans; squash produces squash; spiritual produces spiritual; corruption produces corruption. It's the simple law of sowing and reaping.

In today's text, the principle of sowing and reaping is demonstrated in Jacob's life. After stealing Esau's birthright and blessing, Jacob fled to escape Esau's death threats (Gen 27:41–46). He went to Abraham's original home country, because they still had family there (Gen

> *You reap what you sow.*

28:1–29:2). Jacob didn't realize it, but he was going to learn the first rule of reaping and sowing; you reap what you sow.

Interestingly, Jacob's journey actually began with promise. After Isaac had prayed a blessing over him, Jacob began his journey to Haran (Gen 28:1–5). Early in the journey, Jacob came upon a good place to stay the night. That night, Jacob had an unusual dream in which God spoke to him, "I am the LORD, the God of Abraham your father and the God of Isaac. The land on which you lie I will give to you and to your offspring . . . in you and your offspring shall all the families of the earth be blessed. Behold, I . . . will bring you back to this land (Gen 28:13–15)." As Jacob traveled, his deceitful past must have seemed like a distant memory. The first law of sowing and reaping would reveal itself as soon as he settled in Haran, however.

When he arrived he met a young woman named Rachel, who was a cousin. Rachel was the daughter of his uncle Laban, Rebekah's brother (Gen 29:1–14). Laban and Jacob struck a deal—Jacob would work for Laban, and Laban would provide room and board. Soon after, Jacob fell in love with Rachel, and he contracted with Laban to work seven years to pay the dowry to marry her (Gen 29:15–20). On their wedding night, however, Laban deceived Jacob and substituted Rachel's sister Leah as his wife (Gen 29:21–26). For the first time in his life, Jacob was the recipient of a vicious, deceitful scheme. He harvested the first fruit of his deceitful past.

As a result, Laban and Jacob struck another agreement whereby Rachel would also become his wife, but Jacob had to agree to work an additional seven years for Laban. At this point, Jacob had a full house that included Leah, with her handmaiden Zilpah, and Rachael, with her handmaiden Bilhah (Gen 29:27–30). In the span of a

Day 20

week, Jacob began to understand the second principle of sowing and reaping: you reap more than you sow.

Corn is a great example of this principle. A farmer plants one kernel of corn in the ground, and it will produce a corn stalk. That stalk doesn't produce some additional kernels of corn. Rather, a corn stalk may have two or three ears of corn, and each ear produces dozens of kernels. It's a consistent principle in farm life—you reap more than you sow.

Certainly, Jacob got much more than he'd sown. He tricked Esau out of the birthright, and in return, Laban had tricked him out of his bride. The score seems fairly even at that point. Jacob's harvest was just beginning, however. Genesis 29:31–30:24 is a tale of love, hate, jealously, and intrigue. By the end of his second, seven–year contract, Jacob had four wives and eleven sons. He probably had some daughters that aren't mentioned in the text as well.

During the years of their partnership, Laban and Jacob deceived, stole, and cheated one another. The seeds of Jacob's deceit had produced a full harvest of deceit, frustration, trickery, and turmoil in his life; turmoil that lasted more than fourteen years (Gen 30:25–42). At the end of his contract, Jacob wanted to take his large family back to his own country. Finally, Laban and Jacob decided to part ways, and they made a covenant of peace in the mountains of Gilead (Gen 31:43–53).

Jacob's harvest of corruption abruptly ended at this point of his life. We're told that he offered God a sacrifice before he began his journey home (Gen 31:54). The text continues, "Jacob went on his way, and the angels of God met him. And when Jacob saw them he said, 'This is God's camp!' So he called the name of that place Mahanaim (Gen 32:1–2)." It appears that Jacob's heart was not only turning back toward the land of his father, but also it was turning back toward the God of his father.

Here we find the third principle of sowing and reaping: surprises sometimes happen. God was still at work in spite of Jacob's deceit. When we read about the births of

> *God can work through all of our circumstances and choices, even the foolish ones that lead to his discipline, and turn them into something wonderful and beautiful.*

Jacob's children in Genesis 29 and 30, we realize that Jacob's sons became the heads of the Jewish national families, the 12 tribes of Israel.

While we've been focused on Jacob's deceptions, God has been orchestrating a surprise: a nation has begun. A twelfth son remains to be born, and it will be decades before the family truly comes together. It will be centuries before a centralized nation arises from this family. Still, God's surprise was that the seeds of the nation were sown in Jacob's family. Jacob would one day reap another harvest—one that would remove the label of deceiver and replace it with national patriarch.

Jacob reaped what he had sown, but through it all, God created the family that would become the nation of Israel, his chosen people. This give us hope, no matter what circumstances we may face in our own lives. God can work through all of our circumstances and choices, even the foolish ones that lead to his discipline, and turn them into something wonderful and beautiful. As the apostle Paul wrote, "And we know that for those who love God all things work together for good, for those who are called according to his purpose (Rom 8:28)."

Day 20

Food for Thought

Have you ever felt like you've done some things that God could never forgive? Do you ever wonder if the circumstances of your life prohibit you from loving and serving God? These may be common human feelings, but they don't reflect the truth of Scripture. Like Jacob, God has a purpose for your life that only you can accomplish. While we do reap what we've sown, it's great to know that God can intervene to bring forgiveness, healing, and mercy, and in doing so, create something magnificent in us!

Faith in Action

The Bible has much to say about sowing and reaping. Read Galatians 6:7–8. Every day you're either sowing seeds that are pleasing to God or seeds that are displeasing to God. If you live in a self-indulgent way, you will risk the harvest of deceit and discipline. But if you live in a Spirit-controlled way, you will reap a harvest of truth and blessing. Sow good seeds today for the glory of God.

Prayer

When you pray today, be honest with God about the kind of seeds you've been sowing through your life. If you've been pursuing your own goals and agendas, confess that to God. Ask God to empower you through the Spirit so that you can sow good seeds today, and ask God to send you a harvest of blessing.

Day 21

Jacob's Return

Genesis 32:1–35:29

Homecomings are a big deal in the southern region of the United States. We have them at schools; we have them at churches; we have them in families. We have them as part of Southern Gospel singings, Nashville country music shows, and TV show retrospectives. Homecomings are important. A homecoming means that someone has been away and is now returning. It's a return to family. The return means a renewal of old acquaintances, and it may stir up of old feelings, both good and bad. A homecoming can be both nostalgic and terrifying at the same time.

Jacob's return to Canaan was no different. He was nostalgic about returning to the home of his father (Gen 30:25). Yet, he was terrified of his brother Esau, whom he'd cheated out of the family birthright (Gen 32:7). Jacob was a nervous wreck. He was worried for his family and herds as well as his own life (Gen 32:8, 11). Jacob's return would result in either sorrow or success. As he turned his back on Laban, he had no idea which outcome awaited him.

One thing we know—whatever lay ahead for Jacob, God was going to be in the middle of it. After all, God told Jacob to return to the land of his father (Gen 31:3). When he left Laban, "Jacob went on his way, and the angels of God met him (Gen 32:1)." Jacob prayed when he neared Esau's location (Gen 32:9–12). Then, amazingly, Jacob wrestled with God while he waited for his morning meeting

> *Returning to God means renewing our passion for God.*

with Esau (Gen 32:24–32). The word "wrestle" literally means, "to raise the dust." That night, Jacob got down and dirty with God. He refused to let go of God until God blessed him. Then, after Jacob and Esau met, Jacob erected an altar and called it "God is the God of Israel (Gen 33:20)."

Jacob's newfound obedience to God, which resulted in his return to his homeland, catches us off guard. For more than fourteen years Jacob was with Laban in a foreign country. During that time, we read nothing about his spiritual inclinations. The text is virtually silent about his relationship with the God during those years. But as God began to draw Jacob homeward, we see his heart returning to God as well. Jacob developed a renewed desire to know God and obey his will.

There are several lessons we can learn from this episode in Jacob's life. First, returning to God means renewing our passion for God. Jacob modeled that principle. So did King David. David pleaded to God, "Renew a right spirit within in me (Ps 51:10)." David needed a renewed passion for God following his sin with Bathsheba. When we sin, we must return to fellowship with God as well, and it will always require us to renew a passionate relationship with him.

In the New Testament, the apostle Paul challenged the Ephesian Church to pursue this renewed passion. He wrote, "Put off your old self, which belongs to your former manner of life and is corrupt through deceitful desires, and be renewed in the spirit of your minds (Eph 4:22–23)." The renewed mind is focused on the things of God and not focused on the passions of a deceitful heart. Jacob, it seems, had reached the end of his deceitful days, and he was returning not only to the land of his father but also to the God of his father. He had a renewed passion for God, and God desires the same response from us.

Day 21

Second, returning to God means removing any idols from our lives. At one point, God prompted Jacob to return to Bethel, the place where God had revealed himself first to Jacob (Gen 35:7). Before going to Bethel, however, something remarkable happened. Jacob commanded his family to put away any foreign gods in their possessions (Gen 35:1–4). The text concludes, "So they gave to Jacob all the foreign gods that they had, and the rings that were in their ears. Jacob hid them under the Terebinth tree that was near Shechem (Gen 35:4)."

God desired a close relationship with men and women from the beginning of creation. God was the creator; people were his creation. Adam and Eve walked together in the Garden of Eden. By the time of Jacob, however, man had abandoned the creator in favor of his creation. These false gods were man–made creations. Why would anyone want to worship anything other than the creator God himself?

In the future, Jacob's descendant Moses would hear God say, "You shall have no other gods before me (Ex 20:3)." The Hebrew word for "before me" literally means "face." God was saying, "You cannot have anything in my face," or "You cannot have anything between you and me." Jacob learned and obeyed that lesson long before it was ever included in the Ten Commandments.

Sadly, we may choose to create idols and erect them in place of God. The list is long, but those idols include work, family, money, education, lust, addiction, and countless other manifestations of pride. Anything that takes God's place in our lives is an idol "before him." When we return to God we must remove idols between God and us.

Third, returning to God includes the consistent worship of God. Not only did Jacob return to a passionate relationship with God and remove the idols from his family, but also Jacob returned to

> *Returning to God means removing any idols from our lives.*

> *Returning to God includes the consistent worship of God.*

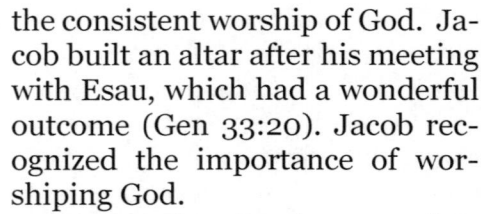

the consistent worship of God. Jacob built an altar after his meeting with Esau, which had a wonderful outcome (Gen 33:20). Jacob recognized the importance of worshiping God.

Later, when Jacob returned to Bethel, the Bible says, "He built an altar and called the place El–bethel (Gen 35:7)." Jacob created a place to offer sacrifices and worship God. While there, Jacob had one of the most significant experiences of his life; God appeared and changed his name to "Israel," which means "God prevails." No longer would Jacob be reminded of his supplanting, deceitful past. After Bethel, he would always be known as "God Prevails."

Jacob responded to his name change by worshiping God. The text says, "And Jacob set up a pillar in the place where he had spoken with him, a pillar of stone. He poured out a drink offering on it and poured oil on it (Gen 35:14)." Jacob had been with God and responded with worship. Returning to God means returning to the consistent worship of God.

Jacob's return to God is nothing short of amazing, and it gives me hope too. No matter what may be happening in my life, I can always return to a close relationship with God. It reminds me of the words of the classic hymn written by William J. Kirkpatrick:

I've wandered far away from God, now I'm coming home
The paths of sin too long I've trod, Lord I'm coming home
I've wasted many precious years, now I'm coming home
I now repent with bitter tears, Lord I'm coming home
I'm tired of sin and straying Lord, now I'm coming home

Day 21

I'll trust Thy love, believe Thy word, Lord I'm coming home
My soul is sick, my heart is sore, now I'm coming home
My strength renew, my hope restore, Lord I'm coming home
Coming home, coming home never more to roam
Open wide thine arms of love, Lord I'm coming home.

Food for Thought

One of our biggest obstacles to spiritual growth is our propensity for erecting idols in our hearts. How is your heart today? Is God on the throne of your life or has something taken his place? Generally, this happens gradually in our lives, and often the things that replace God aren't sinful—they're just in the wrong place in our heart. God welcomed Jacob home, and he is the same today—he is always ready to welcome us home!

Faith in Action

Reading 30 Days to Genesis (and the other books in this series) is a great way to cultivate the daily habit of worship. When we spend some time in personal devotion each day it helps protect us from erecting idols in our lives. Today, look for an opportunity to share what God's teaching you with someone else. Perhaps God will use you to encourage them to become worshipers too!

Prayer

When you worship through prayer today, talk with God about anything in your heart that has the potential to become an idol. Express gratitude for God's good gifts in your life. Then commit to love and worship God more than the gifts he gives you. Finally, ask God to help you live as a worshiper today in every way.

Day 22

A View of the Land

Genesis 36:1–37:1
& Hebrews 11:8–16

Isn't it funny how obvious details can be overlooked? One summer I spent almost two months on an archaeological excavation. While there, I allowed my beard to grow. It was fully grown in by the time I returned to the States. As you might imagine, my wife and I were excited to see one another. As I got out of the car, she ran and jumped into my arms. We hugged and laughed, enjoying the moment. We even kissed, but she never even noticed my beard. It was only later that she exclaimed, "Wait! You have a beard!"

Obviously, I had the beard during our whole reunion, but my wife didn't notice it, even though it was as clear as the nose on my face. She overlooked the obvious. A similar thing happens in the book of Genesis. As we read the stories of creation, the fall, the flood, and the call of Abraham and his descendants, we may miss a critical component—the importance of land. It's obvious, but we usually read over it, oblivious to its significance.

Genesis speaks of land early in creation. "The LORD God formed the man of dust from the ground and breathed into his nostrils the breath of life, and the man became a living creature. And the LORD God planted a garden in Eden, in the east, and there he put the man whom he had formed (Gen 2:7–8)." Not only was the man created from

> *The land of Canaan was a promised place.*

the ground, God created a place on that land for him to live. It was the Garden of Eden.

After Adam and Eve sinned, God drove them out of that amazing garden as part of their discipline. "Therefore the LORD God sent him out from the garden of Eden to work the ground from which he was taken (Gen 3:23)." The land is an obvious character in the narrative. Yet, we miss it.

In today's text, Jacob and Esau make some important decisions about living in the land of Canaan. The story of Abraham began in the heart of the Ancient Near East, in a region connecting three continents: Africa, Asia, and Europe. More specifically, when first we met Abraham, he was living in Mesopotamia. Mesopotamia means "land between the rivers," and it refers specifically to the Euphrates and Tigris rivers. Mesopotamia is important in the Bible for several reasons: the Garden of Eden was probably there, the tower of Babel was there, many Mesopotamian kings are mentioned in the Bible, the Jewish exiles were taken there when Jerusalem was destroyed, and it was the setting for the books of Ezekiel, Esther, Daniel, Ezra, and Nehemiah. Additionally, it was the homeland of Abraham. Today, Mesopotamia is primarily comprised of the countries of Iraq and Syria.

In Genesis 12:1 we read, "Now the LORD said to Abram, 'Go from your country and your kindred and your father's house to the land that I will show you (Gen 13:12).'" Once there, God said to Abraham, "Lift up your eyes and look from the place where you are . . . for all the land you see I will give it to you and to your offspring forever (Gen 13:14–15)." There are twelve passages in Genesis that mention the land in connection with the Abrahamic covenant. As you can see, the land has been attached to God's covenant with Israel from the very beginning, and it will be until the end of time.

Day 22

Today, we discover that Esau was leaving Canaan. "Then Esau took his wives, his sons, his daughters, and all the persons of his household, his cattle and all his animals, and all his goods which he had gained in the land of Canaan, and went to a country away from the presence of his brother Jacob (Gen 36:6)." In contrast we read, "Jacob dwelt in the land where his father was a stranger, in the land of Canaan (Gen 37:1)." The brothers made different decisions about this land of promise. Let's discover what God said about this Promised Land.

First, we learn that the land of Canaan was a promised place. God said to Jacob, "The land that I gave to Abraham and Isaac, I will give to you and I will give the land to your offspring after you (Gen 35:12)." The land embraced by Jacob was a promised land. God had promised the land to his father and grandfather before him. Now, God had passed along the inheritance of the land to Jacob.

Second, we learn is that the land was a temporary place. Notice what the author said about Jacob's choice to remain in the land: "Jacob lived in the land of his father's sojourning, in the land of Canaan (Gen 37:1)." The author of Hebrews described Abraham's situation similarly. "By faith he went to live in the land of promise, as in a foreign land, living in tents with Isaac and Jacob, heirs with him of the same promise, for he was looking forward to the city that has foundations, whose designer and builder is God (Heb 11:9–10)."

Third, we learn that the land was a typological place. Abraham knew that the land had a geographical location. But for him, it was so much more. It was the place that God had promised him, and as such, it was the place where God would meet him. Abraham knew he was just a sojourner in Canaan (Gen 37:1). He believed that the ultimate fulfillment of the land promise would be the place where God dwelled; a place with foundations,

> *The land was a temporary place.*

> *The land of promise in Genesis has become a type for our understanding and longing for heaven.*

a place built by God himself. Consequently, the geographical land promised to Abraham became a type of heaven.

This typology is seen throughout the New Testament as well, and it has taken root in the church's songs of praise. Think of these titles: "There's a Land that is Fairer than Day;" "I am Bound for the Promised Land;" "We're Marching to Zion;" "Beulah Land," and "I Can Only Imagine." The land of promise in Genesis has become a type for our understanding and longing for heaven.

Jesus explained this concept to his disciples in this way, "In my Father's house are many rooms. If it were not so, would I have told you that I go to prepare a place for you? And if I go and prepare a place for you, I will come again and will take you to myself, that where I am you may be also (Jn 14:2–3)." The land Abraham sought, and the one about which Jesus taught, is God's place. It's a place prepared by God for his people.

The apostle John saw it too. He wrote, "And I saw the holy city, New Jerusalem, coming down out of heaven from God, prepared as a bride adorned for her husband. And I heard a loud voice from the throne saying, 'Behold, the dwelling place of God is with man. He will dwell with them, and they will be his people, and God himself will be with them as their God (Rev 21:2–3).'"

God has always had a place for his people. It began in the Garden of Eden. The promise of a land for God's people was given to Abraham. Esau spurned that land, but Jacob embraced it. And although the promise of the geographical land for Israel remains intact, Christians continue to look and long for the promised land of God.

Day 22

Food for Thought

Is there a special place or piece of land that has special significance for you? Did you grow up on a farm or have a favorite get away at the beach or the mountains? What memories does that place evoke in your mind? Pause to reflect on the promises of God to give you an eternal place with him.

Faith in Action

Read the following texts about heaven: Rev 1:10–19; Rev 21, John 14:1ff; Heb 13:13–14; 2 Pet 3:13–14; 1 Cor 15. As you go through your day, meditate on the future that God has in store for you.

Prayer

When you pray today, talk with God about your forever future with him. If you have a relationship with Jesus, God is preparing a place for you in heaven. You don't have to live in fear of death, because death has lost power over you. Thank God for his promise of eternal life.

Day 23

Joseph's Peril

Genesis 37:2–38:30

Back in 1983, the Eurythmics had a hit song called "Sweet Dreams (Are Made of This)." The lyrics say:

*Sweet Dreams are made of this.
Who am I to disagree?
I've traveled the world and the seven seas
Everybody is looking for something.*

Dreams are mysterious and personal. When we dream at night, our brains are sorting through all of the images of the day, in order to catalogue them within our deeper memory. Often, these images connect with our past experiences to create either fun or fearful dreams. When we dream during the day, however, we're often considering decisions and their future implications for our lives. In both instances, the dreams are ours alone.

As the song's lyrics continue, they emphasize the transitory nature of life. No matter where you travel on this planet, you will encounter people who are chasing their dreams, even if they don't know what they really are. We begin the Toledoth of Joseph in Genesis 37, and dreams will play an important part in the story. We learn much about Joseph in the early verses of chapter 37: he was 17, worked as a shepherd, was favored by his father Jacob (who gave him a beautiful cloak), was a tattle–tale,

> *God's plan of salvation is often misunderstood.*

and was hated by his brothers because of it (Gen 37:2–4). Joseph was also a dreamer.

Dreams were considered important in the ancient near east where Jacob and his family lived. When a commoner had a dream, the dream was viewed as a personal message, but when a king had a dream, the dream was believed to have implications for the nation and its people. As a result, kings had dream interpreters as part of their governments; these interpreters were called diviners.

The nation of Israel also acknowledged that God could choose to communicate through dreams. In the Bible, however, diviners of dreams were classified among sorcerers and mediums. In Israel, accepting the interpretation of dreams was only permissible when God's direct involvement in the interpretation could be affirmed. As a result, Israel preserved no standard, formalized literature about the interpretation of dreams.

As a rule, the interpretation of dreams was to be received with caution. Dreamers and dreams were to be tested in the same way as prophets and their prophecies (Deut 13:1–5). We discover two famous dreamers and interpreters of dreams in the Old Testament: Joseph (Gen 37–41) and Daniel (Dan 2, 4). God empowered both men to interpret dreams.

In today's text, Joseph had two dreams. We don't learn until later that God gave Joseph the dreams to foreshadow his plans. Years would pass before Joseph or his family would fully recognize this. Ultimately, he would recognize that God had initiated a plan for keeping both his family and a nation alive, and he had employed dreams as the communication device for revealing his salvation plan. Joseph declared, "God meant it for good, to bring it about that many people should be kept alive, as they are today (Gen 50:20)." We learn much about God's plan of

Day 23

salvation throughout the story of Joseph.

First, we learn that God's plan of salvation is often misunderstood. Joseph's dreams appeared to be the bragging claims of a spoiled child. Joseph's father and brothers didn't understand the dreams. After all, neither did Joseph. God was revealing his plan of salvation, but nobody in Joseph's family understood it.

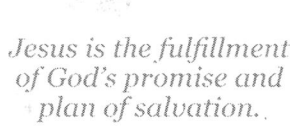

> *Jesus is the fulfillment of God's promise and plan of salvation.*

Jesus is the fulfillment of God's promise and plan of salvation. Yet, he was terribly misunderstood by those around him during his ministry. The religious elite mistook him as a religious heretic. The Romans judged him to be an insurrectionist. Jesus' own disciples misunderstood his purpose until after his crucifixion and resurrection. The apostle Paul wrote, "But we impart a secret and hidden wisdom of God, which God decreed before the ages for our glory." None of the rulers of this age understood this, for if they had, they would not have crucified the Lord of glory (1 Cor 2:7–8). God's plan of salvation is often misunderstood.

Second, we learn that God's plan of salvation often reveals itself in unexpected ways. Joseph was one of Jacob's youngest sons, and his father favored him. He was probably spoiled rotten. His brothers sold him to slave traders who sold him in Egypt as a slave. Ultimately, he ended up in prison. How could God turn all those negatives into positives? God's salvation came in an unexpected way, despite all of the obstacles.

> *God's plan of salvation often reveals itself in unexpected ways.*

The same was true with Jesus. He was from a humble family. He was born in a stable in tiny Bethlehem, and he grew up in Nazareth, a small, rural town in Galilee. Jesus wasn't a Pharisee, Sadducee, or Essene; neither was he a trained Rabbi. God's Savior wasn't what the people expected—Jesus looked much different than the Jewish concept of Messiah.

> God's plan of salvation is motivated by love.

God is so much bigger than our expectations. He is the creator of the universe. He understands all of the events of time and how they can be woven into a beautiful tapestry of salvation history. God controls that history and gives us glimpses into it. Often those glimpses reveal things that are more complex than our minds can comprehend.

Third, we learn that God's plan of salvation is motivated by love. It would take Joseph most of his adult life to realize this. Joseph was sold as a slave to an Egyptian named Potiphar. Potiphar's wife lied about him and had him thrown into prison. Once there, the very people he'd helped, abandoned him. During those years, it must have been very difficult for Joseph to recognize God's love and plan. When his brothers came to Egypt in search of help, however, the pieces of the puzzle began to fall into place. Joseph had matured during his years in Egypt, so he could say, "As for you, you meant evil against me, but God meant it for good, to bring it about that many people should be kept alive, as they are today (Gen 50:20)."

Once again we see the similarities to Jesus' life and death. Both the Roman and Jewish leaders meant to destroy Jesus; yet, God meant it for good. God's plan of salvation was motivated by his love for mankind. Paul wrote, "But God, being rich in mercy, because of the great love with which he loved us, even when we were dead in our trespasses, made us alive together with Christ—by grace you have been saved (Eph 2:4–5)."

> God's plan of salvation originated with God himself.

Day 23

Fourth, we learn that God's plan of salvation originated with God himself. From the very beginning, God intended the events in Joseph's life to be a part of his plan of salvation. God gave Joseph his dreams. God allowed Joseph to become so spoiled that his brothers would want to sell him into slavery. God allowed Joseph's hardships in Egypt to position him for his rise to prominence—a rise that would save his family and the nation of Egypt in their time of need. God was the originator of this amazing plan.

> *God's amazing plan of salvation through Jesus, though often misunderstood, is the greatest indicator of God's love for his world.*

God originated the plan of salvation through Jesus as well. Paul write, God "saved us and called us to a holy calling, not because of our works but because of his own purpose and grace, which he gave us in Christ Jesus before the ages began, and which now has been manifested through the appearing of our Savior Christ Jesus, who abolished death and brought life and immortality to light through the gospel (2 Tim 1:9–10)." God's amazing plan of salvation through Jesus, though often misunderstood, is the greatest indicator of God's love for his world.

30 Days to Genesis

Food for Thought

Has God ever acted in your life in an unexpected way? How did God use that circumstance for good in your life? Ponder the greatness of a God who promises that "for those who love God all things work together for good, for those who are called according to his purpose (Rom 8:28)."

Faith in Action

God doesn't speak to us through dreams anymore, but he does speak through his Word. Read Ephesians 1:3–14. Make a list of all of the things we receive when we commit our lives to Christ. Pay careful attention to the description of how God works out his will in our lives (v. 11–14).

Prayer

As you pray today, reflect on the way God has worked in your life. Remember his provision, in both good times and bad, and worship him in a spirit of gratitude. If you're struggling in a difficult season, commit that situation to God and surrender to his will. You may not know how, but God will certainly use it for good in your life.

Day 24

Prosperity and the Slave

Genesis 39:1–41:57

"Want more money in your bank account? Send in $100 a month, and God's heart will be moved toward you. Then, you will prosper and grow wealthy." How many times have we heard appeals like this from misguided and disingenuous TV preachers? These charlatans prey upon naïve people who believe that wealth is a sign of God's blessing. That is bad theology, however. On one hand, people who are financially prosperous but care very little about the things of God surround us. On the other hand, we know of many people who love and serve God but have little in the way of financial resources. As a result, we cannot claim that obedience to God always results in financial prosperity.

The story of Joseph is a prosperity story. But the prosperity of Joseph is not linked exclusively to personal wealth. In Gen 39–41, we see how faith and prosperity actually work together in a biblical, holistic way. It will become obvious that financial success may be a gift of God's blessing, but biblical prosperity is not limited to one's finances. Today we will learn five truths about a prosperous life.

First, God prospers us by overcoming our difficult circumstances (Gen 37 and 39:2). Consider Joseph's situation. As a young man, Joseph was captured by his broth-

> *God prospers us by overcoming our difficult circumstances.*

ers, thrown into a cistern, sold to slave traders, taken to Egypt and sold to Potiphar, a captain of Pharaoh's guard (Gen 37). We are told in Genesis 39:2, "The Lord was with Joseph, and he became a successful man, and he was in the house of his Egyptian master." Did you catch that? God made Joseph prosperous in spite of his difficult circumstances. Joseph's story teaches us that God will bless us even when we face difficult situations, whether they're on the job, in school, at home, at church, or anywhere else. God can prosper us through it.

Second, God prospers us by being our defense (Gen 39:6–21). As time passed, Potiphar's wife began to desire Joseph; he was a handsome young man, and she wanted to have sex with him. When Joseph rejected her, she falsely claimed that Joseph attempted to rape her. Potiphar's "anger was kindled," and he took Joseph and "put him into the prison (Gen 39:19–20)."

At first glance it's difficult to find anything prosperous about being framed and thrown into prison. But the text says, "But the LORD was with Joseph and showed him steadfast love and gave him favor in the sight of the keeper of the prison. And the keeper of the prison put Joseph in charge of all the prisoners who were in the prison. Whatever was done there, he was the one who did it. The keeper of the prison paid no attention to anything that was in Joseph's charge, because the LORD was with him. And whatever he did, the LORD made it succeed (Gen 39:21–23)." Joseph prospered even though he didn't make a dime—God was his defense.

> *God prospers us by being our defense.*

Third, God prospers us by directing our steps (Gen 40). After Joseph interpreted the dream of

Day 24

Pharaoh's cupbearer, he promised to remember Joseph once he was freed from prison. The cupbearer regained his position and "placed the cup in Pharaoh's hand (Gen 40:21)." Yet, we are told, "The chief cupbearer did not remember Joseph but forgot him (Gen 40:23)."

> *God prospers us by directing our steps.*

Two years later, Pharaoh had some troubling dreams. When no one else could interpret them, the cupbearer remembered Joseph and told Pharaoh about him (Gen 41:1–13). When Pharaoh heard about Joseph we're told, "Then Pharaoh sent and called Joseph, and they quickly brought him out of the pit. And when he had shaved himself and changed his clothes, he came in before Pharaoh (Gen 41:14)." While men were forgetting Joseph, God was directing his steps. Once again God prospered him.

Fourth, God prospers us by removing obstacles from our lives. Pharaoh told Joseph his dreams and asked him to interpret them. Joseph responded, "God has revealed to Pharaoh what he is about to do (Gen 41:25)." When Pharaoh heard the interpretation of his dream he said, "Since God has shown you all this, there is none so discerning and wise as you are. . . . See, I have set you over all the land of Egypt (Gen 41:39, 41)." God prospered Joseph and raised him from the status of slave to that of his most trusted advisor.

> *God prospers us by removing obstacles from our lives.*

God prospered Joseph despite all of the difficult circumstances he had faced. As a result, Joseph gave his sons names to remind him of God's favor. We read, "Joseph called the name of the firstborn Manasseh. 'For,' he said, 'God has made me forget all my hardship and all my father's house.'

> *God prospers by giving us himself.*

The name of the second he called Ephraim, 'For God has made me fruitful in the land of my affliction (Gen 41:51–52).'" Joseph recognized that his prosperity came from God.

Fifth, God prospers by giving us himself. It was God who was with Joseph in Potiphar's house; it was God who blessed him while he was in prison; it was God who gave him the interpretation of Pharaoh's dreams; it was God who allowed him to forget the pain his brothers caused him; it was God who made Joseph fruitful in the land of his affliction. God was working all things together for good for Joseph, and he does the same for all of his children.

The Bible is filled with stories about God's power to overcome the mistreatment, lies, and hardships suffered by his people. This is how God prospers his people. Consider Paul's words of encouragement to the Christians in Rome,

> If God is for us, who can be against us? He who did not spare his own Son but gave him up for us all, how will he not also with him graciously give us all things? Who shall bring any charge . . . Who is to condemn? . . . Who shall separate us from the love of Christ? Shall tribulation, or distress, or persecution, or famine, or nakedness, or danger, or sword? . . . No, in all these things we are more than conquerors through him who loved us (Rom 8:31–37).

God prospers his children in many ways, and occasionally, he may choose to prosper them financially, too. Regardless of the form his blessing takes, God is working on your behalf today, in both your good and difficult situations, so that you can be fruitful as you walk through this challenging thing called life.

Day 24

Food for Thought God prospers his people in ways that exceed financial prosperity. While financial prosperity is sometimes a gift from the Lord, the biblical idea of prosperity extends far beyond mere financial blessing. Reflect on the ways God has prospered you—you life, health, family, education, career, church, and friends. Have you paused to be grateful lately for the way that God has prospered you in these areas? Has God favored you with financial provision? Honestly, if you live in America you've been given greater financial blessing than more than 90% of the people on earth. Are you obeying God in your resources? Are you tithing weekly to your church in obedience to God's word? Are you being generous with your other resources to bless those around you for the sake of the gospel?

Faith in Action Today, focus on being grateful for the ways that God has prospered you. To help with this, carry an object in your pocket today. This can be a small cross, a fifty cent piece, or even a small stone. Every time you feel it in your pocket, let it prompt you to be grateful to God for one of the ways he has prospered you. You will be amazed at how praising can transform your day!

Prayer As you pray today, thank God for working on your behalf today. Thank him for prospering your with his good gifts, including the gift of himself through Jesus. Thank him for your salvation. Ask him to make you aware of the good gifts he brings into your life today!

Day 25

Extending God's Salvation

Genesis 42:1–45:28

Athletes take great pride in preparation, because they know why they're preparing. Athletes realize that without it, they won't be ready on game day. That preparation comes at a cost, however. Athletes put their bodies through all sorts of painful and difficult exercises. They push themselves to extreme limits so that they won't be embarrassed when its game time. They know that the game is coming, so they prepare for it. As a result, they will be able to perform at their highest levels.

In today's text, Joseph was confronted by a similar situation. He wasn't preparing to play a game, however. Rather, he was preparing to save a nation. Genesis 42–45 contains the concluding episode of Joseph's dream cycle. As you recall, his story began in Genesis 37. There we were introduced to Joseph as a young man who misused his dreams for self–glorification and self–promotion. His actions, along with his status as Jacob's favorite son, aroused the anger and jealousy of his older brothers. After being sold into slavery and rising to a place of prominence in Pharaoh's government, Joseph found himself, quite unexpectedly, in the company of his brothers once again.

We read, "Moreover, all the earth came to Egypt to Joseph to buy grain, because the famine was severe over all the earth (Gen 41:57)." Like countless others, Jacob's

> *God orchestrates our futures.*

family was in need of food because of the famine. Finally, Joseph's story begins to come into sharp focus. God knew that a famine would crush Canaan, so he positioned Joseph to be his instrument of salvation for Jacob's family when the time came. We read, "So ten of Joseph's brothers went down to buy grain in Egypt (Gen 42:3). As Joseph encounters his brothers, the ones who produced so much pain and suffering in his life, we are left to wonder how he would respond. Would Joseph be consumed by anger and take revenge against them?

The drama is heightened when we are told, "Joseph saw his brothers and recognized them, but he treated them like strangers and spoke roughly to them. And Joseph recognized his brothers, but they did not recognize him (Gen 42:7–8)." Four times the author uses the verb "to recognize" in these two verses. The ESV translates the passive occurrence like this: "treated them like strangers." A better translation of this Hebrew construction is this: "he was unrecognized to them." Further, we're told, "Joseph remembered the dreams that he had dreamed of them (Gen 42:9)." A perfect revenge scenario was in place. Since Joseph recognized them, but was unrecognized by them, he could exact his revenge and none would be the wiser.

Instead of enacting revenge upon his brothers, however, Joseph set in motion a series of events that would help him discern the condition of his brothers' hearts. He wanted to know if they had changed for the better over the years. So, Joseph arrested them and held them in prison for three days. Then, he told them that they were free to go home with the grain that they needed, but Simeon had to remain in prison. To get more food in the future, and to secure the release of their brother Simeon, they had to bring their youngest brother when they returned. Joseph's brothers were distraught; they knew that their father Ja-

Day 25

cob refused to let Benjamin travel them—he wasn't about to lose another favored son. They began to speak to one another in Hebrew, unaware that Joseph could understand them. They said, "In truth we are guilty concerning our brother, in that we saw the distress of his soul, when he begged us and we did not listen. That is why this distress has come upon us (Gen 42:21)." When Joseph heard their words, he "turned away from them and wept (Gen 42:24)."

We aren't told why Joseph wept, but most likely he wept because their words brought back the horror of that day. He remembered begging them not to sell him to the slavers and watching their heartless response as he was shackled and led away. Now the tables were turned. They were the ones in distress, pleading for Joseph change his mind. Would he act like his brothers once had?

The brothers returned home and told Jacob about Simeon's plight, but he refused to allow Benjamin to leave. However, "The famine was severe in the land (Gen 43:1)." Desperate times call for desperate measures. Eventually, their need for food was so great that Jacob relented and allowed them to return to Egypt for more grain—Benjamin in tow.

The brothers were terrified of Joseph. "So they went up to the steward of Joseph's house and spoke with him at the door of the house (Gen 43:19)." After being reassured by the steward, they were taken in to see Joseph, who asked about their father. They replied, "'Your servant our father is well; he is still alive.' And they bowed their heads and prostrated themselves (Gen 43:28)." When Joseph saw Benjamin, he was so overcome with emotion that he fled to his chamber to weep.

Once again we are left to wonder what was in Joseph's heart. I imagine when he saw Benjamin he was reminded of the day

> *God prepares his people for their roles in his kingdom.*

147

> *God's plan has always been to use redeemed people as conduits of his grace.*

when he was his father's favorite son. Also, I'm sure that he was filled with love for his baby brother. Further, I think Joseph was overcome with emotion when he realized that God had revealed the meaning of those early dreams. In his distant past, God had shown Joseph what was to come and how he would use him to save his family. Finally, those dreams had become a reality. Joseph's heart melted with love—love for his family and love for his great God, who had orchestrated all things together for good. How could he act spitefully and hatefully towards his brothers when he knew that God had directed his entire life for this moment?

After studying these chapters, I think there are three helpful principles for our lives. First, God orchestrated Joseph's future. From the moment we're introduced to Joseph, God was giving him dreams about his future. Like an elite athlete in training camp, the hardships in Joseph's life were preparing him to accomplish God's purpose. Then, when the time was perfect, Joseph was in a position to save his family from the famine.

Similarly, God orchestrates our futures too. John wrote in his first letter, "God is greater than our heart, and he knows everything (1 John 3:20)." God said to Isaiah, "I declared them to you from of old, before they came to pass I announced them to you (Is 48:5)." God is all knowing. He knew Joseph's future, and he knows ours.

Second, God prepared Joseph for his future. All of the tragic events in Joseph's life shaped him into the compassionate leader he became. God allowed difficulties to invade his life, yet he continued to favor him. Joseph's growth through those difficulties gave him the fortitude and compassion to act as he did. God used all of those difficulties to mold, shape, and prepare Joseph for his future task.

Day 25

The Bible is filled with stories of people that God prepared for important tasks. Esther (Es 4:14) and David (1 Sam 17:31–37) are great examples. But God is still preparing people today. Paul wrote to the Ephesians, "And he gave the apostles, the prophets, the evangelists, the shepherds and teachers, to equip the saints for the work of ministry, for building up the body of Christ, until we all attain to the unity of the faith and of the knowledge of the Son of God, to mature manhood, to the measure of the stature of the fullness of Christ (Eph 4:11–13). God prepares his people for their roles in his kingdom.

Third, God used Joseph as an ambassador of salvation. God's plan has always been to use redeemed people as conduits of his grace. Jesus commanded his disciples to go and make more disciples (Mat 28:18–20). Paul told the Corinthians, "In Christ God was reconciling the world to himself, not counting their trespasses against them, and entrusting to us the message of reconciliation. Therefore, we are ambassadors for Christ, God making his appeal through us (2 Cor 5:19–20)." God wants every believer, including you and me, to be his ambassadors of the gospel.

Joseph was at the place and time to accomplish God's work in the world. God had prepared him, and he followed God and fulfilled his mission. Today, God is preparing you for your kingdom mission. He has you in the perfect place to accomplish your task of serving as an ambassador of the gospel. The proper response is up to you!

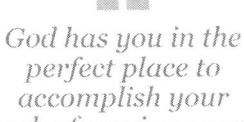

> *God has you in the perfect place to accomplish your task of serving as an ambassador of the gospel.*

30 Days to Genesis

Food for Thought

God uses all of the circumstances in our lives to prepare us to serve him—he wastes none of them. You are who you are, and where you are today, because of his sovereign plans. The question is this: are you being faithful to your calling to be an ambassador of the gospel? Are you using your one, precious, God–given life to be a conduit of salvation for the people around you? Of, have you been mired in disappointment when you look at the circumstances of your life? Joseph could have spent his life in despair—he had it far tougher than you or I ever will. Instead, he trusted God and followed him all the days of his life. What will you choose today?

Faith in Action

Read Psalm 139:13–18, 24. These verses reveal that God had a purpose for your life long before he created you. How can this encourage us to live as ambassadors of his grace today? Rather than allow yourself to be discouraged today, look for someone to bless in Jesus' name today. And, if God gives you an opportunity to share the gospel today—take it!

Prayer

When you pray today, talk with God about the journey of your life to this point. First, praise God for all of the ways he's shown you favor. Second, talk with him about the difficult circumstances in your life. Ask for the wisdom to understand them and to leverage them into conversations about the gospel with those who may be experiencing the same kind of things.

Day 26

Following God Into Difficult Tasks

Genesis 46:1–34

Following God will often require you to attempt difficult tasks. After all, God asked Abraham to sacrifice Isaac. Moses was sent to lead the people of Israel out of Egypt. God led Joshua to drive out the enemy and settle the land of Canaan. David fought with Goliath. Jeremiah was sent to preach to people who hated his message. Stephen was stoned to death for preaching that gospel to the Jews, while God sent Paul to preach the gospel of Jesus to the Gentiles. Of course, God may never call us to perform tasks as difficult as these. Yet, following Christ always comes with a cost (Lk 9:23–26). God had a final plan for Jacob at the end of his life, and it would be hard too. Today, let's look at how Jacob accomplished it.

Jacob had never expected to get this news—Joseph was still alive? Joseph was still alive! The news was so overwhelming that "his heart became numb, for he did not believe them (Gen 45:25–26)." But the news was true. Not only was Joseph still alive, but also he wanted to bring Jacob and his entire family to Egypt. Jacob rejoiced greatly (Gen 45:27–28)!

The thought of moving to Egypt produced a dilemma for Jacob, however. How could he move his entire family to Egypt when God had told him to settle in the land of Canaan? Jacob's heart and mind must have been troubled

> Yet, following Christ always comes with a cost.

as he packed up his life to journey to Egypt. He desperately wanted to see his long-lost son, and his family was in desperate need of food. He couldn't stay where he was while his son and food were in Egypt. Still, Canaan was God's chosen and promised place for his family. In spite of this, Jacob chose to follow God, and his response has provided us an example for following God through difficult tasks.

First, Jacob worshiped God. We are told that before he left for Egypt, Jacob "took his journey with all that he had and came to Beersheba, and offered sacrifices to the God of his father Isaac (Gen 46:1)." You will recall that Beersheba was the place from which Jacob left for Haran to choose a wife all those years ago (Gen 28). It was from Beersheba that he would also leave for Egypt. Jacob worshiped when he arrived in Beersheba. After all, worship is always the best way to begin a difficult task.

Understanding why Jacob worshiped is crucial for us. Worship establishes a proper attitude toward God. As we offer up sacrifices of worship to God, we are admitting that God is greater than us. He is sovereign over all things, and we need his help in our lives. We must always begin a difficult task by worshiping God.

Second, Jacob listened to God. God spoke to him while he worshiped. We read, "And God spoke to Israel in visions of the night and said, 'Jacob, Jacob.' And he said, 'Here I am' (Gen 46:2)." Before attempting a difficult task, we must worship God and be sensitive to the Holy Spirit's work in our hearts. We will not hear the audible voice of God like Jacob did, but the Spirit will speak to us through God's Word to direct our steps (Jn 16:7–15).

> We must always begin a difficult task by worshiping God.

Day 26

Third, Jacob understood God's plan. God assured Jacob that he was doing the right thing by going to Egypt. In Genesis 46:3–4, God provides us with several key truths to remember when attempting the difficult tasks in our own lives. Initially, God reminded Jacob that he was in control. He stated simply, "I am God (46:3)." This phase reminded Jacob that he could trust God in every situation—even the hard ones. This same truth applies to our lives as well. God is always in control of our circumstances.

> *God is always in control of our circumstances.*

Next, God reminded Jacob that there was no reason to fear. He said, "Do not be afraid to go down to Egypt . . . I myself will go down with you to Egypt (Gen 46:3–4)." Jacob had no reason to be afraid, because he wasn't going to Egypt alone; God was going along for the ride. What a great truth! When God gives you a difficult task, he will walk with you; you're never on your own (Heb 13:5).

Finally, God reminded Jacob he had a customized plan for his life. God told Jacob, "Do not be afraid to go down to Egypt, for there I will make you into a great nation. I myself will go down with you to Egypt, and I will also bring you up again, and Joseph's hand shall close your eyes (Gen 46:3–4)." God had a very specific plan for Jacob that he wanted him to understand. Jacob would go to Egypt, his family would flourish there, and he would die there, with Joseph by his side. God has specific plans for us too. The psalmist tells us, "The steps of a man are established by the LORD, when he delights in his way (Ps 37:23)." Remember as you serve that God is in control, we don't need to live in fear, and God will accomplish his will in our lives.

Fourth, Jacob obeyed God. We read, "Then Jacob set out from Beersheba . . . and came into Egypt (Gen 46:5–6)." Obedience is the way that we display our faith in God and his plans for our lives. Jacob obeyed God and moved to

> *When God gives you a difficult task, he will walk with you; you're never on your own.*

Egypt. For us, obeying God might mean going to pray with a friend, witness to a neighbor, or leave on a short-term mission trip. James, the brother of Jesus said, "Faith by itself, if it does not have works, is dead (James 2:17)." Once we understand God's kingdom plans for our lives, we must obey him.

Fifth, and finally, Jacob trusted God. The wording of Genesis 46:7 is interesting; it hints at God's larger redemptive plan for the world. Jacob wasn't the only person going into Egypt. The text reads, "All his offspring he brought with him into Egypt (Gen 46:7)." The Hebrew word translated "offspring" is the same word that is translated "seed" in Genesis 3:15. The word speaks of Jacob's descendants; among which is the promised one who will one day bruise the head of the serpent.

Further, God had told Jacob, "The land that I gave to Abraham and Isaac I will give to you, and I will give the land to your offspring after you (Gen 35:12)." Again, this is the word for "seed." Jacob was taking his family to Egypt, but God had promised them the land they were leaving. The people would have to return to the Promised Land for God's promises to be fulfilled. In this story we learn that God was not only overseeing Jacob's personal plans, but also he was orchestrating his larger redemptive plan for the world; a plan to send a Savior to crush the serpent and defeat sin and death.

Similarly, God may call us to attempt difficult tasks for him. So, when you think God is leading you into a difficult task, remember to worship God, listen to God, attempt to understand God's plan, obey God's plan, and trust God on your journey.

> *Obedience is the way that we display our faith in God and his plans for our lives.*

Day 26

Food for Thought — *The Bible reveals that God has a kingdom purpose for each of us. We accomplish that task through active participation in God's church. God calls us to participate in his church through regular corporate worship, using our gifts in ministry, demonstrating faithfulness in our tithes and offerings, and living on mission through the gospel (Eph 4:11–16). This is true for you, me, and every other believer on earth. Are you obeying this call of God on your life? If not, what area do you need to submit to God today?*

Have you ever wondered if God has a big task for your life? I've found that the best way to be prepared for a big plan is to be faithful and obedient in the small things first. Start by spending some time with God every day. Working through the 30 Days to the Bible devotional commentaries is a great way to do this. Next, be faithful in the body life of your church, looking for ways to use your spiritual gifts for God's glory. Finally, live with a missional worldview, striving to point people to Jesus through the gospel. If God has a big task for you, he will reveal it while you're being faithful in these areas. — *Faith in Action*

Prayer

In your prayer time today, talk with God about his plans for your life. If you've let some of your spiritual tasks suffer by disconnecting from God's church, confess those sins and commit to be obedient. Then, ask God to use your life to point others toward a life of obedience through Christ. Finally, tell God you're ready to attempt any task he gives you—no matter how hard it may be.

Day 27

Learning to Bloom Where Planted

Genesis 47:1–31

My wife loves flowers, and while she loves to receive them on special occasions, she prefers them in a garden. We have had flower gardens everywhere we've lived. She has purchased flowers to plant, used cuttings from friends and family to grow them, and started flowers from seeds and bulbs. She will work with them, sweat over them, and threaten me if I approach them.

The other day, I saw some flowers growing near our heating and air unit. The blooms had long since passed, and the branches were impeding the airflow. So, I did what any good husband would do—I mowed them down. Hey— one can't be too cautious with such things!

Obviously, I didn't risk telling her for a few days. Finally, my better judgment took over, and I told her about her flowers; I knew she would eventually see it anyway. To be honest, she took it much better than I expected. She was disappointed for a few days, and I have survived to tell the tale.

As it turns out, however, my grandmother, who died many years ago, gave those flowers to us; my wife had them for more than ten years. Impressed, I asked her how many of our other plants had survived our multi–state moves. One Hosta plant, which my wife got from my aunt, has survived four moves to four towns—with four totally different soil types! In each of those settings, the plant not only survived, it thrived. In each location the plant had to be divided into new plants several times. On top of that, my wife has given cuttings from that plant to others, and they've flourished every time. It might even survive being mowed. Stay tuned.

Like my wife's Hosta, Joseph found a way to flourish in every difficult circumstance he faced. In other words, he learned to bloom where he was planted. In today's text, Joseph provides us with an example of how to make the most of every situation, no matter how challenging it might be.

First, Joseph provided for his family's needs (47:1–12). Early in his life, Joseph's brothers had sold him into slavery. He could have resented his family to the point that he cared very little for them, if at all. After all, they had ruined his life, or so it seemed. Yet, he didn't choose to act harshly towards them when they appeared before him. Instead, Joseph chose to flourish where he was planted. We're told, "And Joseph provided his father, his brothers, and all his father's household with food, according to the number of their dependents (Gen 47:12)."

Joseph was living out the truth we find recorded throughout Scripture. Paul told Timothy, "But if anyone does not provide for his relatives, and especially for members of his household, he has denied the faith and is worse than an unbeliever (1 Tim 5:8)." Here, then, is biblical principle: we should provide for our families' needs rather than resenting them.

Second, Joseph did excellent work in every task he was assigned, whether it was in Potiphar's house, working for the prison warden, or serving as Pharaoh's right hand man (Gen 47:13–26). Joseph found himself in an important position. He had spent seven years rationing food in order to prepare for an impending famine. Now, the famine was in full force. In order to please Pharaoh, Joseph had to be shrewd. Pharaoh expected him to do what was best for the Egyptian kingdom—Joseph's life depended on it.

Day 27

As the famine progressed, the people of Egypt ran out of money. Yet, the grain bins were full because of Joseph's planning. As a result, Joseph devised a plan that would allow the people to trade their animals and livestock for food. Eventually, the people had sold all their livestock to Pharaoh. They had nothing else with which to buy food.

So, Joseph devised another plan. This time the people were required to sell their land to Pharaoh to purchase grain. Eventually, all the land had been sold to Pharaoh. Now what would happen? The people had nothing left with which to buy grain. Finally, Joseph purchased the people themselves. While this sounds cruel, it was the only thing the people had left to sell to Pharaoh. The people said, "You have saved our lives; may it please my lord, we will be servants to Pharaoh (Gen 47:25)."

Third, Joseph was sympathetic towards the Egyptian people. The people were at the mercy of Pharaoh and Joseph after selling everything they possessed. Joseph could've been cruel, but he wasn't. Instead, Joseph chose to be sympathetic towards them.

As the famine neared its end, Joseph provided the people with seed to plant. At the time of the harvest, the people were to return one–fifth of all the harvest to Pharaoh. In one wise step, Joseph profited both Pharaoh and the people. Joseph's sympathy alleviated some of the pain of a catastrophic situation. The people could rebuild their lives while honoring their contracts with Pharaoh.

The apostle Paul had much to say about work in the New Testament. He wrote, "Whatever you do, work heartily, as for the Lord and not for men, knowing that from the Lord you will receive the inheritance as your reward (Col 3:23–24)." Joseph lived this principle despite the difficult circumstances of his life. Joseph al-

> *Whatever you do, work heartily, as for the Lord and not for men, knowing that from the Lord you will receive the inheritance as your reward.*

> When we find ourselves in difficult situations, we have two options: we can wither away or choose to bloom where we're planted. What will you do?

ways labored as if working for the Lord. In doing so, Joseph bloomed where he'd been planted.

Fourth, Joseph managed Jacob's estate (Gen 47:27–31). Not only did Joseph provide for his family's present needs, but also he promised to care for Jacob's estate. Jacob didn't want to be buried in Egypt, so he made Joseph promise to take him back to the Promised Land. Joseph agreed and served as the executor of Jacob's will. Later we will read that Joseph fulfilled his father's wishes with great pomp and circumstance. Once again, Joseph bloomed where he was planted.

Remember that plant I mowed down? It survived and thrived (much to my relief!). Often, we may feel as if life has mowed us down. When we find ourselves in difficult situations, we have two options: we can wither away or choose to bloom where we're planted. What will you do?

Day 27

Food for Thought The last few days have provided us with insights for dealing with adversity. Joseph managed to walk through adversity with great success. How would you? Are you experiencing a difficult time in your life? If so, are you wilting or blooming? Are you trusting God or trying to work it out on your own? If you're in a good season of life, it's a good time to grow in your knowledge of how to respond to adversity the next time you face it.

Faith in Action

Spend a few moments thinking about the different areas of responsibility in your life. Are you blooming in those areas of your life? If not, why? Are you doing your best work for the glory of God, regardless of the circumstances? If not, commit to make one positive adjustment in that area of your life today.

Prayer

In your prayer time today, talk with God about the different areas of responsibility in your life (heart issues, relationships, job, school, church, etc.). If you're wilting in one of those areas, talk with God about it. Then, commit to do your best in that area for his glory. Also, if you're in a good place, ask God to help you encourage someone else who may be struggling to bloom where they're planted.

Day 28

Facing Two Directions

Genesis 48:1–50:13

Sadly, human beings die. Consider Hebrews 9:27, "It is appointed for man to die once." We know that fact by instinct and observation, although it's not easy to contemplate. In modern times, Elisabeth Kübler–Ross' book On Death and Dying has become the standard work on the psychological effects people experience when facing death. She lists those attitudes as denial, isolation, anger, bargaining, depression, and acceptance. Kübler–Ross states that once people reach the acceptance stage, they have the ability to realistically discuss their impending deaths.

In today's reading, we discover that Jacob's death was imminent (Gen 48:3–4). He took comfort in his faith and the process of arranging for his burial and the affairs of his family following his death (Gen 49:29). We can learn a great deal from the way Jacob responded during this time and make application to our own situations as we face our own mortality and that of friends or family.

First, Jacob remembered life's blessings as he looked to the past (Gen 48:1–7). This is a great way for people to find joy as death approaches. It's comforting to remember all of God's good gifts in life, because it reminds us of God's faithfulness through both good and challenging times.

> *It's comforting to remember all of God's good gifts in life, because it reminds us of God's faithfulness through both good and challenging times.*

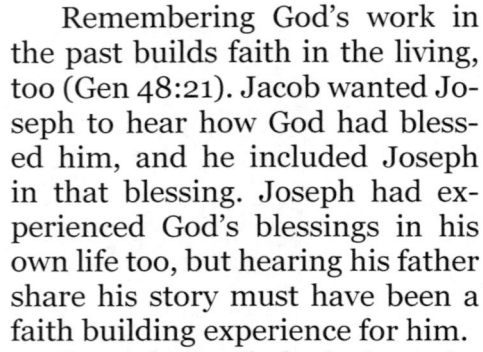

Remembering God's work in the past builds faith in the living, too (Gen 48:21). Jacob wanted Joseph to hear how God had blessed him, and he included Joseph in that blessing. Joseph had experienced God's blessings in his own life too, but hearing his father share his story must have been a faith building experience for him.

Second, Jacob looked to the future. He shaped his legacy before his death (Gen 48:8–49:28). He did this by speaking blessings into the lives of Joseph's sons, Ephraim and Manasseh. As Joseph brought his sons to his father, he positioned his youngest son on Jacob's left and his oldest son on Jacob's right (Gen 48:13). During this time in history, the right hand was the place of honor and blessing. Jacob did something that was unexpected, however. Mirroring his own life, he crossed his hands and placed the hand of blessing on Joseph's youngest son. When Joseph saw it, he attempted to reposition Jacob's hands so that Manasseh, his eldest son, would receive the greater blessing (Gen 48:14–18); Jacob would have none of it. He explained to Joseph, "I know, my son, I know. He also shall become a people, and he also shall be great. Nevertheless, his younger brother shall be greater than he, and his offspring shall become a multitude of nations (Gen 48:19)."

It's easy to understand Jacob's affinity for Joseph's younger son. Both Joseph and Benjamin had been his favorites; they were also his youngest sons. Still, at the end of his life, Jacob orchestrated events so that Joseph's youngest son Ephraim would receive the larger blessing.

In Genesis 49:1–33, Jacob further shaped his legacy by pronouncing blessings upon all of his other sons. Some of those blessings sound more like judgments, while others reflect great favor. These comments should not be viewed

Day 28

as absolute predictions. After all, only God can foretell the future. Still, Jacob used these comments to help shape how his sons would live and behave in the future. We're told, "All these are the twelve tribes of Israel. This is what their father said to them as he blessed them, blessing each with the blessing suitable to him (Gen 49:28)." The blessings reflected Jacob's desires as much as anything else—he was shaping his legacy.

We don't speak blessings over our children in the same way they did in Jacob's day. However, it's not uncommon in our day for the dying to explain their burial and estate plans to members of their families. They will often reminisce about their lives as well. It's a natural, human response to impending death.

In the movie Lonesome Dove, Captain Call goes to great cost and effort to bury his friend Augustus McRae in Texas. Gus was dying in Montana when he made this request of Call. Call's epic journey is a powerful episode in the movie—it highlights his loyalty to his friend. After Gus is buried, an exhausted Captain Call remarks, "Well, Gus, there you go. I guess this will teach me to be more careful about what I promise people in the future." Like Gus, Jacob shaped his legacy by receiving a deathbed promise.

In the final event of his life, Jacob expressed his desire to be removed from Egypt. In Genesis 49:29, Jacob told his sons exactly where to bury him in Canaan. Then, Genesis 50:12 says, "And his sons did unto him according as he commanded them." Jacob prearranged his funeral service and burial before he died.

While some may think it's morbid, prearranging after–death events removes many decisions from your loved ones. I've been a pastor for almost three decades now, and I've seen both sides of the situation—those who've made

> *When facing death must look in two directions; to the past for comfort and faith and to the future for shaping our legacy and guiding the decisions of our families.*

165

plans before their deaths and those who haven't. I can assure you that planning is better. My own grandmother prearranged the funeral speakers, songs, and order of service. She also boxed up her funeral clothes so that her children didn't have to worry about selecting them while they were grieving. While sad, that was incredible blessing to her children.

Dying is difficult to face, but it's something everyone must do. Jacob's example is helpful, especially when God gives us advance notice of our deaths. When facing death must look in two directions; to the past for comfort and faith and to the future for shaping our legacy and guiding the decisions of our families.

Day 28

Food for Thought

One day all of us will die. What will your legacy be? To leave a legacy you must first live a legacy. Do you have a personal relationship with Jesus Christ (if you're not sure, please read "Finding L.I.F.E. in Jesus" at the end of this book). Are you building a life of faith to transfer to your children? Have you given thought to legacy planning and giving as it relates to your personal estate? If not, why?

Faith in Action

It's never too early to think about your own death. Honestly, living with an awareness of our own mortality is one of the best ways to get the most out of life—you quickly realize that life is too precious to waste. Do you have life insurance for your family? Do you have a will? Have you identified guardians for your children in the event of an early death? Have you given any thought to your funeral arrangements? If you're lacking in some of these important areas, take steps to correct it immediately.

Prayer

When you spend time with God in prayer today, talk with him about the brevity of life. The book of James says it's brief, like a vapor. Ask God for the wisdom to live well and die well. Ask God to help you make the necessary plans so that when you die, your family will know that you loved them. Finally, ask God to help you leave a legacy of faith in Christ that will impact your family for generations to come.

Day 29

Buried in Egypt, Longing for Home

Genesis 50:14–26

We had just loaded the van for our 10–hour journey. Our youth group was leaving for a mission trip to partner with a new church plant. There was a buzz of excitement as we loaded up and headed out. We'd driven no further than 15 miles when a mom called me from one of the other vehicles.

"We need to stop," she said.

"What?" I replied. "Surely nobody has to use the bathroom already."

Her voice dropped to a whisper. "Trust me, we just need to stop."

I pulled off at the next exit and went back to her car. When I leaned down at the window, I could hear one of our young ladies sobbing as if someone had died. I looked at her and asked, "What's wrong?"

She looked at me with tears streaming down her cheeks and replied, "I want my momma!"

We were 20 minutes into our journey and already homesickness had overwhelmed this young girl. It was both sad and funny at the same time. The driver of her vehicle and I chatted with her for some length of time in an attempt consolation. After all, we wanted her to experience this mission trip. Eventually she calmed down and decided to stay with us. She had a great week too!

> *When God moves in our lives, he does so within the complexity of our unique stories, and he is still able to accomplish his will.*

I was amazed by the power of homesickness. Of course, homesickness is about neither home nor sickness. Rather, it's separation anxiety wrapped in nostalgia. Homesickness can occur in people of all ages, genders, and nationalities. When we're separated from familiar things and familiar people, we begin to feel out of place. The lack of familiarity makes us nostalgic for what we know. In the worst instances, homesickness can lead to clinical depression and despair. Yet, for most people, the emotions subside over time.

In our text today, Joseph was nearing death. That's when homesickness hit him. In Genesis 50:25 we're told, "Then Joseph made the sons of Israel swear, saying, 'God will surely visit you, and you shall carry up my bones from here.'" Then, the book of Genesis ends in this very strange way, "So Joseph died, being 110 years old. They embalmed him, and he was put in a coffin in Egypt (Gen 50:26)."

Joseph was homesick for God's Promised Land. By the time of his death, he'd been away from Canaan since he was a young boy. He'd grown more and more nostalgic for home as he aged. He would never go home, but he longed for his body to be buried there when God brought his people up out of Egypt (Gen 50:24). Genesis ends with Joseph buried in Egypt. Make no mistake, however; Joseph knew his dreams would come true.

Although Joseph was homesick and longing for the Promised Land, he didn't despair over dying in Egypt. Joseph had a strong faith in God, and it helped him avoid the things that cause hopelessness to take root. We can learn some principles from Joseph in these concluding verses of Genesis.

First, Joseph understood the complexity of God's plans (Gen 50:15–21). Joseph's brothers were afraid when Jacob died. They wondered if Joseph had been waiting to

Day 29

take revenge against them. Sure, he had every right to be angry with them after they'd shipped him off to Egypt. Instead, Joseph was a model of kindness.

That's because Joseph understood something that his brothers didn't. He said, "'Do not fear, for am I in the place of God? As for you, you meant evil against me, but God meant it for good, to bring it about that many people should be kept alive, as they are today. So do not fear; I will provide for you and your little ones.' Thus he comforted them and spoke kindly to them (Gen 50:19–21)." Joseph understood that all of the hardships he'd encountered at the hand of his brothers were a part of God's plan, and God's plans are complex.

As a rule, we want our lives to be simple, but that isn't reality—life is never simple. Our stories interact with the stories of others. When God moves in our lives, he does so within the complexity of our unique stories, and he is still able to accomplish his will. God said, "For as the heavens are higher than the earth, so are my ways higher than your ways and my thoughts than your thoughts (Isaiah 55:8–9)." Accepting this truth will help protect us from despair. Life's complexities shouldn't make us despondent. Joseph's story teaches us that God accomplishes his plans despite the chaos that plagues our world.

Second, Joseph understood that God's promises are certain. As a result, he could overcome his homesickness by trusting God. Joseph said, "God will visit you and bring you up out of this land to the land that he swore to Abraham, to Isaac, and to Jacob (Gen 50:24)." There was no doubt in this statement. God would visit and bring them up. Joseph was so confident in God's promises that he made his brothers swear to take his bones to the Promised Land when it happened. For Joseph this wasn't an "if;" it was a "when."

> *God accomplishes his plans despite the chaos that plagues our world.*

> *Believing God's promises gives us hope—a confident expectation—for both life and death.*

The book of Hebrews helps us understand the certainty of God's promises to Abraham. We're told, For when God made a promise to Abraham, since he had no one greater by whom to swear, he swore by himself . . . For people swear by something greater than themselves, and in all their disputes an oath is final for confirmation. So when God desired to show more convincingly to the heirs of the promise the unchangeable character of his purpose, he guaranteed it with an oath, so that by two unchangeable things, in which it is impossible for God to lie, we who have fled for refuge might have strong encouragement to hold fast to the hope set before us. We have this as a sure and steadfast anchor of the soul (Heb 6:13, 16–19a).

The same is true for us. Believing God's promises gives us hope—a confident expectation—for both life and death. That hope is an anchor for our souls. Joseph had that. He anchored his soul to the promises of God, even as he faced death. He believed God's promises, because repeatedly he'd seen God keep his word. He knew God's promises, and he acted on them, even in death. We, too, must learn to trust God's promises in all of the complexities of our own lives. It's comforting to know that God's promises are true, and he is faithful to keep them.

No matter how complicated your life might be today, God's promises for you are certain. For instance, God promises to meet our needs when we live with generous hearts. Paul wrote, "And my God will supply every need of yours according to his riches in glory in Christ Jesus (Phil 4:19)." Don't despair over your finances—God can provide for you no matter how complex your situation may be.

Here's another promise. "Be content with what you have, for he has said, 'I will never leave you nor forsake you.' So we can confidently say, 'The Lord is my helper; I will not fear; what can man do to me? (Heb 13:5b–6).'" Are

Day 29

you facing a situation that makes you afraid? You don't have to face it alone; God will never leave you.

Want one more promise? "Humble yourselves, therefore, under the mighty hand of God so that at the proper time he may exalt you, casting all your anxieties on him, because he cares for you (1 Pet 5:6–7)." It's arrogant to try and navigate the complexities of life without God's help. Instead, God promises to care for us and help us if we'll trust him. How do we do this? We cast our anxieties upon him. After all, he's the only one who can handle them anyway. When we do, he promises to use his might to make sense of the senseless in our lives.

God's promises remain certain in the midst of life's complexities. Don't yield to hopelessness or despair. Trust God with your life—he can handle it.

It's comforting to know that God's promises are true, and he is faithful to keep them.

30 Days to Genesis

Food for Thought — You've been learning about the life of Joseph this week. Think about all of the complexities in his family that God had to navigate to accomplish his will. Yet, God succeeded in his plans. Now, think about the complexities that revolve around your life. Are you facing circumstances that are difficult? Are you wondering what to do next? Remember, God has promised to work out his will in your life too, regardless of complexities involved (Rom 8:28; Phil 1:6).

Faith in Action — Take some note cards and write down the three promises from today's devotion (Phil 4:19; Heb 13:5b–6; 1 Pet 5:6–7). Read these verses throughout the day. As you do, remember that God made these promises to you. Then, choose to believe them!

Prayer

When you pray today, talk with God about the complexities of your life. Talk with him about your hopes and fears. Claim the promises that God made you today through his word. Surrender your life and your plans to God's will. Then, watch how he directs your steps today.

Day 30

A Certain God for Uncertain Times

Exodus 1:1–14

On March 21, 1980, the most famous TV cliffhanger of all time aired. That episode of Dallas was titled "A House Divided." In it, an unknown assailant shot J.R. Ewing. For the rest of the year millions of the shows fans pondered the same question: "Who shot J.R.?" The writers' cliffhanger produced a publicity tidal wave. The show's fans eagerly anticipated the answer to the mystery. Dallas' fall premier was titled "Who Done It?," and it became the highest rated show in TV history at that time, drawing more than 80 million American viewers and another 300 million worldwide. Today, it's still the second highest rated TV episode of all time. Because of the success and popularity of the "Who shot J.R.?" mystery, annual cliffhangers became an industry standard for almost every TV drama.

In a similar way, Genesis ends with a cliffhanger. We read Genesis and ask, "That's how Genesis ended? Joseph buried in Egypt? Really? What about Joseph's family? What about his brothers, the fathers of Israel? Surely the author won't leave us hanging like that, right?

Unfortunately, yes. The Book of Genesis intentionally leaves us hanging in mid–story, because it's only the first part of the larger narrative of the Bible. The author wants us to keep reading the story of Joseph's death in Egypt (Gen 50). For our last study in Genesis, let's take a

> *We serve a certain God even in uncertain times, and we must be intentional about sharing that good news with the people around us.*

sneak peek at the resolution of the cliffhanger. Obviously, we can't study the entire story of Exodus here. Instead, let's watch the trailer of Exodus in chapter one.

Interestingly, the story of Joseph's death is told in both Genesis 50 and Exodus one. While Joseph promised his family protection in Egypt in Genesis 50, a future Pharaoh removed it from them in Exodus one.

In Exodus 1:1–5, the author quickly reveals that all of Jacob's descendants were still in Egypt. Time had passed, however. Joseph, his brothers, and that whole generation had long since died. We read, "Then Joseph died, and all his brothers and all that generation (1:6)." The brevity of this statement creates angst and we are compelled to read further.

As we peek into Exodus, we notice two truths about God's people—the nation called Israel. First, they were in a perilous position in Egypt. Years after the death of Joseph "there arose a new king over Egypt, who did not know Joseph." Joseph had long since died, and sadly, nobody in the Egyptian government remembered him.

Further, the new Pharaoh caused the Egyptians to resent the people of Israel. We read, "And he said to his people, 'Behold, the people of Israel are too many and too mighty for us. Come, let us deal shrewdly with them . . . So they ruthlessly made the people of Israel work as slaves (Ex 1:9–10, 13).'"

Then, in an attempt to slow Israel's population growth, Pharaoh gave the Jewish midwives a horrifying command: "When you serve as midwife to the Hebrew women and see them on the birthstool, if it is a son, you shall kill him, but if it is a daughter, she shall live (Ex 1:16)." These were uncertain times, indeed. Yet, the author constantly reminds us that God is certain, even in perilous days.

Day 30

Second, they were in a prosperous position. Despite Pharaoh's evil plans, "The people of Israel were fruitful and increased greatly; they multiplied and grew exceedingly strong, so that the land was filled with them (Ex 1:7)." Then we read, "But the more they were oppressed, the more they multiplied and the more they spread abroad. And the Egyptians were in dread of the people of Israel (Ex 1:12)." God was bringing prosperity to his people even in perilous times.

This happened in part because the midwives refused to obey Pharaoh. "But the midwives feared God and did not do as the king of Egypt commanded them, but let the male children live . . . So God dealt well with the midwives. And the people multiplied and grew very strong. And because the midwives feared God, he gave them families (Ex 1:17, 20–21)." God prospered his people despite the evil intentions of one of the most powerful men on earth.

Certainly, that lesson is one we need today. Our times are perilous and uncertain as well. Natural disasters, dangerous diseases, international terrorism, and a general sense of global unrest have produced stress and fear in our lives. We serve a certain God even in uncertain times, and we must be intentional about sharing that good news with the people around us.

With great skill, the author of Genesis has concluded our study by reminding us that God is certain in our uncertain world. God will protect his people from peril and provide them with his favor, because nothing is impossible for him (Lk 1:37). The abrupt ending of Genesis simply reminds us of where it all began: "In the beginning, God (Gen 1:1)."

> *God will protect his people from peril and provide them with his favor, because nothing is impossible for him.*

30 Days to Genesis

Food for Thought — We live in a crazy world. It's been that way since sin entered the world, however. The Bible is filled with stories about people just like us, who learned to trust God in chaos of life. In every perilous situation, the Bible reminds us that God is constant and certain. His promises are true, and he always keeps them. He is able to overcome any difficult situation in our lives. You may have fears about the future, but they're senseless. God is control, and you can live with hope and peace because he is.

Faith in Action — Today you concluded your 30 day adventure through Genesis. Take some time to review your notes and thoughts over the past 30 days. Then, make a list of the most valuable things God taught you this month (you can write them on the pack page of your book). Review these truths from time to time in your spiritual walk.

Did you like this study? There are other books in this series that cover other books in the Bible. I want to encourage you to get another one and continue the habit of spending time every day with God through Bible study and prayer. Also, consider telling some of your friends about this series. God wants to use it for good in their lives too!

Prayer — As you pray today, reflect on the things God taught you this month. Thank God for loving you enough to give you his word. Ask him to help you live in the reality of his love and purpose for your life. And, commit to trust him in every area of your life—he is certain in uncertain times!

Finding L.I.F.E. in Jesus!

Everyone wants to be happy. The hard part is determining exactly what that means. For some, happiness is defined through relationships. They believe that popularity, a huge friend list on Facebook, and a significant other produces happiness. For others, happiness is defined through success. They believe that personal achievement, a huge number in their bank account, and plenty of expensive toys produces happiness. For still others, happiness is defined through community. They believe that personal growth, a huge impact for societal change, and embracing diversity produces happiness. And these things do—until they don't.

Experiencing happiness is as difficult as catching the greased pig at the county fair. It appears to be right in front of us, but then it slips through our fingers and is gone. Friends, achievement, and personal growth have the potential to bring happiness into our lives, but when our friends disappear, success eludes us, and we realize that we're incapable of self–transformation, happiness is quickly replaced by disillusionment and depression. The problem with pursuing happiness is that it is an emotion that is driven by our circumstances. And let's be honest—we all tend to have more negative than positive experiences in our lives.

So, what's the answer? Should we keep doing the same things while expecting different results, or should we consider what Jesus has to say about finding our purpose for life? If you want to stay on the hamster wheel while you try to catch up to happiness, you can stop reading here. But if you're ready to consider what God wants to do in your life, please read on.

God never promises happiness in the Bible. Are you surprised to hear that? Instead, he promises something much greater—joy. While happiness is an emotion fueled by circumstance, joy is an attitude fueled by God's Spirit. Happiness is self–determined. In other words, I am the sole determiner of whether I'm happy at any given moment. Joy, on the other hand, is God–determined. God has promised to give us joy, and it isn't based on our circumstances—it's based on God's character and promises.

This is why Jesus never talks about giving people happiness. He knew all too well that chasing happiness is like chasing your shadow. You can never catch it. Instead, he talks about giving people life. He said, "I came that they may have life and have it abundantly (Jn 10:10)." Here, Jesus reveals that the thing people really want, whether they know it or not, is abundant life. To have an abundant life means that you are personally satisfied in all areas of your life, and you experience peace and contentment as a result. Jesus' statement also means that we do not have the capacity to create that kind of life for ourselves. Jesus came in order to give it to us. But how? The Bible tells us that achieving this kind of satisfied life requires us to know something about God, ourselves, and the reason for the death and resurrection of Jesus Christ.

First, we must understand God's **love**. The Bible says that God is love (I Jn 4:8), and God created us so that we could know him and experience his love (Gen 1:26–31). God created us to be worshipers and to live forever in the reality of his glory. And, when sin marred his perfect creation, he created a plan to free men and women from its curse. At just the right time in history, God sent his own Son, Jesus, into our world. "For God so loved the world, that he gave his only Son, that whoever believes in him should not perish but have eternal life (Jn 3:16)." It is

Finding L.I.F.E. in Jesus!

God's love that motivates him to restore relationship with those who are separated from him by sin.

Second, we must understand our **isolation**. To be isolated is to be separated from someone, and as a result, to be alone. This is what sin has done to us. It has separated us from the very one we were created to know, love, and worship—God. When Adam and Eve rebelled against God by breaking the lone command he had given them, the entire world was brought under the curse of sin (Gen 3). As a result, God removed them from the Garden of Eden, and their perfect fellowship with God was broken. In an instant, they had become isolated from God because of their sin. From that moment to this, every person born into this world is guilty of sin. The Bible says, "For all have sinned and fall short of the glory of God (Rom 3:23)." Because of this "there is none righteous, no, not one (Rom 3:10)." Further, "The wages of sin is death (Rom 6:23a)." We were created to love and worship God in perfect community, but now because of sin we are isolated from him. Meanwhile, we try to satisfy this desire to know God by pursuing our own happiness, even though we can never hope to attain it. And in doing so, we risk being isolated from God for all eternity.

Third, we must understand our need for **forgiveness.** There is only one way to experience God's love and escape the isolation caused by sin—we must experience God's forgiveness. In spite of sin, God never stopped loving the people he created. He promised Adam and Eve that he would send someone who could fix the problem they had created. When it was time, God sent his own Son, Jesus, to be the world's Savior. This, too, was an act of God's love. The Bible says, "God shows his love for us in that while we were still sinners, Christ died for us (Rom 5:8)." When Jesus died on the cross, he was paying the penalty for our sins (Rom 3:23–26). When God raised Jesus from the dead, it was to demonstrate that forgiveness was available to all who would receive it by faith. Paul explained how this happens in his letter to the Ephesians. "For by grace you have been saved through faith. And this is not your own doing; it is the gift of God, not a result of works, so that no one may boast (Eph 2:8–9)."

The reality is that we cannot experience salvation as a result of our own efforts. We can try to be a good person, go to a church, even give a ton of money to worthy causes—none of these "works" can provide forgiveness. No matter how hard we try, we will always "fall short of the glory of God." That is why we must receive God's offer of forgiveness and salvation by faith. Faith simply means to trust or believe. Salvation requires us to believe that God loves us, that we are isolated from him by our sins, and that his Son Jesus died and was raised to life again to pay the sin debt that we owe God because of our sins. When we take God up on his offer of the gift of salvation, he doesn't just give us forgiveness—he gives us life! The Bible says, "The free gift of God is eternal life in Christ Jesus our Lord (Rom 6:23)."

Fourth, we must understand the **enjoyment** that comes from knowing, loving, and worshiping God. Whether we know it or not, we are slaves to sin until God sets us free (Rom 6:20–23). This was the ultimate reason that God sent his Son, Jesus, to die on the cross for our sins—God sent Jesus so that we could be set free from our sins. Jesus said, "You will know the truth, and the truth will set you free. . . . Everyone who commits sin is a slave to sin. . . . So, if the Son sets you free, you will be free indeed (Jn 8:32–36)." Jesus was teaching us that we must be set free from sin in order to enjoy the life that God has given us—both now and in eternity future. We are set free when we commit our lives to Jesus Christ through faith in his death and resurrection. Then, and only then, will we find joy in the abundant life of Jesus Christ!

So, the question for you is a simple one: Are you ready to experience freedom from sin and the abundant life that Jesus promised you? If so, God is waiting for to talk with him about it (Jer 29:13). Stop right where you are and make this your prayer to God,

Finding L.I.F.E. in Jesus!

"Father in heaven, I know that I'm a sinner. I know that I've done lots of things that displease you and disappoint you. And, I know that I'm isolated from you because of my sin. I know that if I die without knowing you, I will spend forever separated from you in hell. But, I believe that Jesus is your sinless Son, and I believe that he died on the cross for me. I believe that he died to provide a perfect payment for my sin debt. I believe that you raised him from the dead so that I could experience forgiveness for my sins. Right now, Father, I'm asking you to forgive me of my sins and save me. I am receiving your Son Jesus as my personal Lord and Savior. I will follow you the rest of my life. Please give me the joy of a life spent knowing, loving, and worshiping you. I ask these things in Jesus' name, Amen."

If you made the decision to accept Jesus as your Savior today, we want to talk with you! Please contact the people at www.seed–publishing–group.com. We would love to talk with you about your decision and help you with your first steps in following Jesus!

If you enjoyed *30 Days to Genesis*, check out the other books in the *30 Days to the Bible* series.

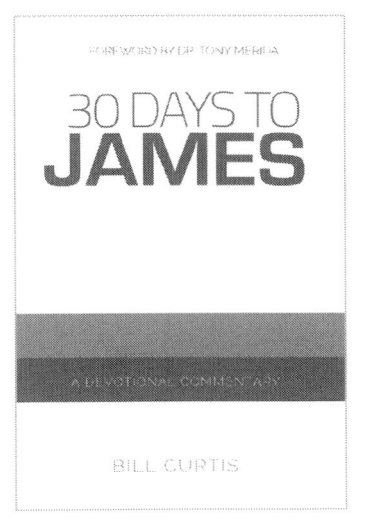

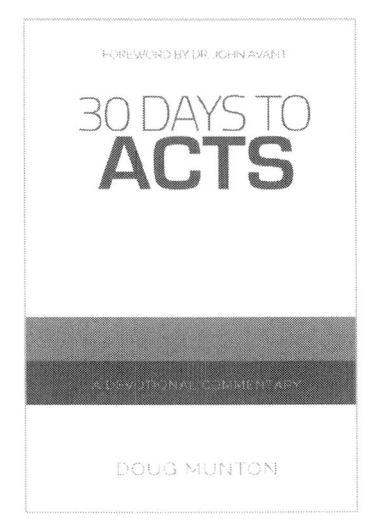

Also from Seed Publishing:

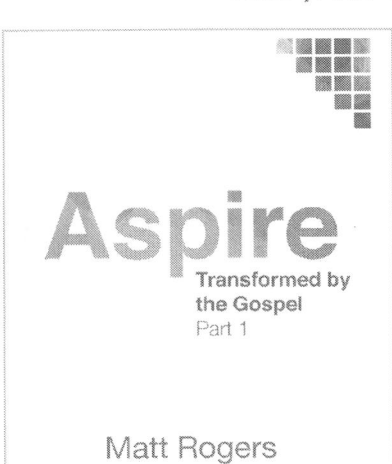

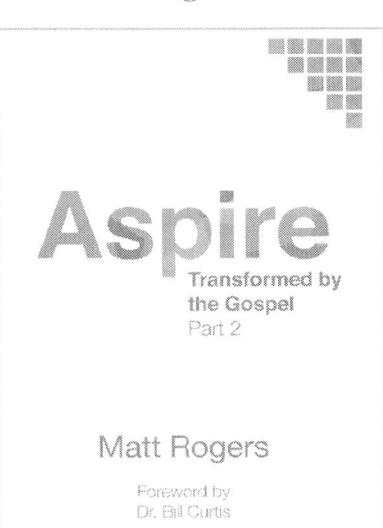

Made in the USA
Charleston, SC
13 January 2017